ENGLISH
INTERIOR
DECORATION
1500-1830

1   The Hall, Blenheim Palace, Oxfordshire: The Saloon, by Sir John Vanbrugh, *circa* 1705.
From a water-colour by W. B. E. Ranken

ENGLISH INTERIOR DECORATION

1500 to 1830

A Study in the
Development of Design

By

MARGARET JOURDAIN

Illustrated from Drawings, Prints and Photographs

B. T. BATSFORD LTD

LONDON   NEW YORK   TORONTO   SYDNEY

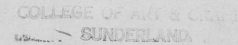

Other works by Margaret Jourdain

ENGLISH DECORATION AND FURNITURE OF THE EARLY RENAISSANCE, 1924

ENGLISH DECORATION AND FURNITURE OF THE LATER XVIIIth CENTURY, 1922

ENGLISH INTERIORS FROM SMALLER HOUSES OF THE
SEVENTEENTH TO THE NINETEENTH CENTURIES, 1923

ENGLISH DECORATIVE PLASTERWORK OF THE RENAISSANCE, 1926

GEORGIAN CABINET-MAKERS, 1939 (In collaboration with R. Edwards)

REGENCY FURNITURE, 1948

THE WORK OF WILLIAM KENT, 1948

FIRST PUBLISHED, 1950

*Made and printed in Great Britain for the publishers B. T. Batsford Ltd., 15 North Audley Street, London, W.1;
122 East 55th Street, New York; 103 St. Clair Avenue West, Toronto; 156 Castlereagh Street, Sydney.
Text by Balding & Mansell Ltd., 4 Snow Hill, London, E.C.1. Plates by Unwin Bros. Ltd., Woking*

PREFACE

THIS work is based on the publishers' Library of Decorative Art, which consisted of four volumes, two on Furniture and on Decoration in the middle period (1640 to 1760) to which were added a volume on the Early Renaissance (1924) and one on the later Classical Revival (1922), in which Decoration and Furniture were treated together. It has been thought advisable to combine the subject of Interior Decoration in this one volume, so that the course of its design may be studied as a whole from the Early Renaissance to the end of the first third of the nineteenth century. Some of the subjects of the older volumes have been used, but a large number of houses have been specially photographed by Mr. A. F. Kersting. Sections have been added on contemporary work in the United States, for purposes of comparative study. For the sake of simplification some of the material on features and detail, including measured drawings, etc., has been omitted. More attention has been given to complete interiors, and to the Regency period, with a section on the revived Gothic of the early nineteenth century. The text has been extensively revised, and in part rewritten with some additions. It is hoped to follow the volume in due course with a similar one on Furniture of the same periods, so that with the two volumes the course of design in Decoration and Furniture can be followed through over three centuries.

M. JOURDAIN

London, Summer, 1950

ACKNOWLEDGMENT

THE publishers wish to express their gratitude to the owners of the houses illustrated for kindly allowing their properties to be photographed and for permission to reproduce the illustrations shown.

For the photographs reproduced the publishers are indebted to Messrs. Country Life Ltd., for Figs. 11, 12, 56, 87, 112, 129, 151, 158, 191 and 192; Mr. Herbert Felton, F.R.P.S., for Figs. 172, 177, 179, 180, 182, and 183; Mr. A. F. Kersting, F.R.P.S., for Figs. 4, 7, 26–28, 30, 41, 51, 52, 62, 64, 65, 70, 72, 75, 76, 78, 79, 82, 83, 89, 91–93, 95–97, 106, 114–122, 124, 130–135, 137, 138, 141–147, 150, 154, 157, 159, 160, 162, 165–167 and 181; the National Buildings Record, for Fig. 193; the Royal Commission on Historical Monuments, for Fig. 29; Mr. Walter Scott, Bradford, Yorkshire, for Figs. 8, 38 and 127; Mr. Reece Winstone, A.R.P.S., Bristol, for Fig. 9.

The originals of the illustrations of American subjects have been kindly collected by Mr. Tom Waterman, who must be thanked for his very friendly co-operation. The copyrights of Figs. 73, 74, 81, 101, 103, 104, 110, 111, 113, 136 and 148 belong to the Historic American Buildings Survey, Library of Congress; of Fig. 44 to Mr. H. Bagby, Richmond, Virginia, of Figs. 71, 80 and 99 to the Frances Benjamin Johnston Arts Club, Washington, D.C.; of Figs. 55 and 102 to the Metropolitan Museum of Art, New York; and of Fig. 109 to Mr. Robert W. Tebbs, New York. Fig. 169 is included by kind permission of Sir Hereward Wake, C.B., C.M.G., D.S.O., from a photograph by the late Mr. John Bean of Northampton. Figs. 170 and 184 are kindly supplied by the Wallpaper Manufacturers Ltd., Manchester.

The majority of Mr. Kersting's photographs have been specially taken for this book; the remainder of the subjects are taken from the publishers' collection.

CONTENTS

PREFACE . . . .
PAGE
v

ACKNOWLEDGMENT . . . .
vi

LIST OF ILLUSTRATIONS . . . .
ix

CHAPTER

I DECORATION OF THE EARLY RENAISSANCE, 1500–1650 . . I

Introduction: The Interior. *The Italian Influence under Henry VIII — The Elizabethan Agricultural and Trading Expansion — The Early Seventeenth-century Building Period — The Reign of Charles I — The Commonwealth*
Foreign Influences: *The Italian Influence — The Influence of the Low Countries — The Jacobean Style — French and Italian Influences in the Reign of Charles I*
Decorative Painting and Colouring: *Wall Paintings — Early Printed Papers — Colour — Paper Hangings*
Woodwork: *Clinker-boarding — Early Tudor Panelling — Linenfold — Medallioned Heads — Late Tudor Panelling — The Orders — Jacobean Wainscot — Construction — Carving — Woods*
Carving: *Decline of Technique in the Early and Middle Tudor Period — The Italian Influence — The Flemish Influence — Carolean Carving*
Inlay: *Inlay of Woods, and of Compressed Shavings — Parqueting*
Plaster: *Design of Plaster — Foreign Sources of Design — Local Centres — Colour Decoration — Ingredients*
Interior Features: *The Staircase — The Chimney-piece — The Interior Porch and Door*
Glazing of Windows: *The Bay Window — The Importation of Glass in the Reign of Elizabeth — Glazing — Ventilating Quarries — Stained and Painted Glass Panels and Medallions*
The Screen

II THE LATE STUART PERIOD, 1650–1720 31

Introduction: The Interior. *The Work of Inigo Jones — The Dutch Influence*
Decorative Painting
Plaster
Wainscot
Wood-Carving
Interior Features: *The Staircase — The Chimney-piece — The Door*

III THE EARLY GEORGIAN PERIOD, 1720–1770 . . . 45

Introduction: The Interior. *The Palladian School — The Decoration of James Gibbs and William Kent — The French, Gothic and Chinese Tastes — Decoration in America*
Decorative Painting: *Kent — Amiconi — Casali — Clermont*
Plasterwork: *The Palladian School of Plasterwork — The Italian Stucco Workers — The Rococo*
Wainscot: *Niches and Alcoves*
Interior Features: *The Staircase — The Chimney-piece — The Door*

IV THE CLASSICAL REVIVAL OF THE LATER EIGHTEENTH CENTURY, 1760–1820 56

Introduction: The Interior. *The Age of Collections — The Work of Robert Adam — Sir William Chambers — The Classical Revival*
Decorative Painters and Designers of Ornament
Plaster Work, Scagliola and Other Decorative Processes: *The Work of Robert Adam — Cast Medallions — Scagliola, Marble and Gilding — Colour Schemes — The Etruscan Style — Marbling and Graining*
Interior Features: *The Hall and Staircase — The Chimney-piece — The Door and Door-case*

V THE REGENCY PERIOD AND REVIVED GOTHIC, 1790–1830 . 73

Introduction: The Interior. *The Work of Henry Holland and Sir John Soane — The Revived Gothic — The Chinese Taste — Decoration in America*
Wall-Hangings: *Textiles — Paper Hangings — Chinese Papers*

INDEX TO TEXT AND ILLUSTRATIONS 79

LIST OF ILLUSTRATIONS

Fig. 1 The Hall, Blenheim Palace, Oxfordshire . . . . . . *Frontispiece*
  Stall Backs, the Convocation House, Oxford. Drawing by J. Gillespie . . . *Page* 8
  Chimney-piece ornament, Boston House, Brentford. From an engraving by Abraham de Bruyn 6
  Wall paintings from Saffron Walden Museum: Seward's End and the Gabriel Hervey House. 11
  The Old Neptune Inn, Ipswich 14
  Room in Upper Floor of House, Norwich. Drawing by W. Curtis Green, R.A. . . 16
  Door from the Norwich House of William Lowth 28

Fig. 2 The Great Chamber, Gilling Castle, Yorkshire . . . . *Between pages 28 and 29*
3 The Oak Room, Badminton, Gloucestershire . . . . . ,, ,,
4 The Cartoon Gallery, Knole, Sevenoaks, Kent . . . . ,, ,,
5 The Oak Parlour, Quenby Hall, Leicestershire . . . . ,, ,,
6 The State Drawing-room, Quenby Hall, Leicestershire . . . ,, ,,
7 The Hall, Hatfield House, Hertfordshire . . . . . ,, ,,
8 The Hall, Montacute House, Somerset . . . . . ,, ,,
9 Plaster Panel in the Hall, Montacute House, Somerset . . . ,, ,,
10 The Long Gallery, Albyns, Essex . . . . . ,, ,,
11 Screen to Kederminster Pew, Langley Marish Church, Buckinghamshire . ,, ,,
12 The Kederminster Library, Langley Marish Church, Buckinghamshire . ,, ,,
13 Crewe Hall, Cheshire. The Great Hall. From a water-colour by Joseph Nash ,, ,,
14 The Dining-room, Forde Abbey, Dorset . . . . . ,, ,,
15 The South Room, Slyfield, Surrey . . . . . ,, ,,
16 The Staircase, Aldermaston, Berkshire . . . . . ,, ,,
17 The West Staircase, Castle Ashby, Northamptonshire . . . ,, ,,
18 Detail of Balustrade, the West Staircase, Castle Ashby . . . ,, ,,
19 The Staircase, Rawdon House, Hoddesdon, Hertfordshire . . . ,, ,,
20 Detail of Carved Panels, the Staircase, Rawdon House . . . ,, ,,
21, 22, 23 Elizabethan Wall Paintings in The White Swan, Stratford-on-Avon ,, ,,
24 The Staircase, Lees Court, Kent . . . . . . ,, ,,
25 Chimney-piece in the Stone Parlour, Lyme Park, Cheshire . . ,, ,,
26 Chimney-piece in the house of Sir Thomas Herbert, Pavement, York . ,, ,,
27 Interior porch, Montacute House, Somerset . . . . ,, ,,
28 The Dining-room, Sudbury Hall, Derbyshire . . . . ,, ,,
29 Upper Stage of the State Room Chimney-piece, Boston House, Brentford ,, ,,
30 Upper Stage of Chimney-piece, Chicheley, Buckinghamshire . . ,, ,,
31 Painted Glass, the Great Chamber, Gilling Castle, Yorkshire . . ,, ,,
32 Upper Stage of the Hall, Lees Court, Kent . . . . *Between pages 44 and 45*
33 The Colonnade Room, Wilton House, Wiltshire . . . . ,, ,,
34 The Double Cube Room, Wilton House, Wiltshire . . . ,, ,,
35 The Single Cube Room, Wilton House, Wiltshire . . . . ,, ,,
36 Staircase, Coleshill, Berkshire . . . . . . ,, ,,
37 The State Bedroom, Powis Castle, Montgomeryshire . . . ,, ,,
38 The Cedar Room, Warwick Castle, Warwickshire . . . . ,, ,,
39 The Dining-room, Dunster Castle, Somerset . . . . ,, ,,
40 The Hall of the Strafford Building, Wentworth Castle, Yorkshire . . ,, ,,

Fig. 41 The Parlour, Sudbury Hall, Derbyshire . . . . . *Between pages 44 and 45*
42 The East Tapestry Room, Wentworth Castle, Yorkshire . . . ,, ,,
43 The Tapestry Room, Castle Howard, Yorkshire . . . . ,, ,,
44 The Dining-room, Kenmore, Fredericksburg, Virginia, U.S.A. . . ,, ,,
45 The Fourth Room, Holyrood House, Edinburgh . . . . ,, ,,
46 The Study, Holme Lacy, Herefordshire . . . . . ,, ,,
47 The Balcony Room, Dyrham Park, Gloucestershire . . . ,, ,,
48 The King's Dining-room, Drayton House, Northamptonshire . . ,, ,,
49 The Tapestry Room, Belton House, Lincolnshire . . . . ,, ,,
50 The Dining-room, Badminton House, Gloucestershire . . . ,, ,,
51 The Billiard Room, Chicheley, Buckinghamshire . . . . ,, ,,
52 The Drawing-room, Chicheley, Buckinghamshire . . . . ,, ,,
53 Coombe Abbey, Warwickshire . . . . . . ,, ,,
54 Coombe Abbey, Warwickshire . . . . . . ,, ,,
55 Drawing-room, Marmion, Virginia, U.S.A. . . . . ,, ,,
56 The Painted Room, Wilsley House, Cranbrook, Kent . . . ,, ,,
57 The Staircase Hall, Stoke Edith, Herefordshire . . . . ,, ,,
58 The Hall, Stoke Edith, Herefordshire . . . . . ,, ,,
59 The Drawing-room, Sudbury Hall, Derbyshire . . . . ,, ,,
60 The Staircase Hall, Brickwall, Northiam, Sussex . . . . ,, ,,
61 The Drawing-room, Denham Place, Buckinghamshire . . . ,, ,,
62 The Staircase, Chicheley, Buckinghamshire . . . . ,, ,,
63 The Staircase at 75 Dean Street, Soho . . . . . ,, ,,
64 The Long Gallery, Sudbury Hall, Derbyshire . . . . ,, ,,
65 The Staircase, Sudbury Hall, Derbyshire . . . . . ,, ,,
66 The Staircase, Tythrop House, Oxfordshire . . . . ,, ,,
67 Scroll Balustrade on the landing, the Staircase, Tythrop House . . ,, ,,
68 Detail of scroll Balustrade, the Staircase, Tythrop House . . ,, ,,
69 The Hall and Staircase, Powis Castle, Montgomeryshire . . ,, ,,
70 The Grand Staircase, Easton Neston, Northamptonshire . . ,, ,,
71 Detail of the North Stair, Tuckahoe, Virginia, U.S.A. . . ,, ,,
72 The Staircase, Chicheley, Buckinghamshire . . . . ,, ,,
73 The Dining-room, Cupola House, North Carolina, U.S.A. . . ,, ,,
74 The Drawing-room, Cupola House, North Carolina, U.S.A. . . ,, ,,
75 The Queen's Bedroom, Sudbury Hall, Derbyshire . . . ,, ,,
76 Doorway at first floor landing, Sudbury Hall, Derbyshire . . ,, ,,
77 Detail of carvings in the Saloon, Lyme Park, Cheshire . . ,, ,,
78 Garniture for a picture, Sudbury Hall, Derbyshire . . . ,, ,,
79 Detail of the carving of the Garniture, Sudbury Hall . . . ,, ,,
80 The Stair and Arch, Sabine Hall, Richmond County, Virginia, U.S.A. . ,, ,,
81 Arched Doorways, Hope Lodge, Whitemarsh, U.S.A. . . ,, ,,
82 The Dining-room, Easton Neston, Northamptonshire . . . ,, ,,
83 The Hall, Ragley, Warwickshire . . . . . . ,, ,,
84 The Marble Parlour, Houghton Hall, Norfolk . . . *Between pages 52 and 53*
85 The Saloon, Holkham Hall, Norfolk . . . . . ,, ,,
86 The Saloon of the Provost's Lodge, Trinity College, Dublin . . ,, ,,
87 The Shell Grotto, Goodwood House, Sussex . . . . ,, ,,
88 The Low Drawing-room, Wentworth Woodhouse, Yorkshire . . ,, ,,
89 The Tapestry Room, Hagley Hall, Worcestershire . . . ,, ,,
90 The Whistle-Jacket Room, Wentworth Woodhouse, Yorkshire . . ,, ,,
91 The Saloon, Hagley Hall, Worcestershire . . . . ,, ,,
92 The Gallery, Hagley Hall, Worcestershire . . . . ,, ,,

Fig. 93 The Entrance Hall, Hagley Hall, Worcestershire . . . *Between pages 52 and 53*
94 The Hall, Ditchley, Oxfordshire . . . . . " "
95 The Octagon Room, Orleans House, Twickenham . . . " "
96 The Ceiling of the Octagon Room, Orleans House, Twickenham . " "
97 Ceiling on the first floor, House of Charity, Soho Square, London . " "
98 Ceiling of the Hall, Ragley Hall, Warwickshire . . . " "
99 The Drawing-room, Brandon, Prince George County, Virginia, U.S.A. " "
100 The Palladian Room, Gunston Hall, Fairfax County, Virginia, U.S.A. . " "
101 Waterman House, Rhode Island, U.S.A. . . . . " "
102 The Drawing-room, Marmion, Virginia, U.S.A. . . . " "
103 Staircase and Arch, Jerathmael Bower's House, Somerset, Massachusetts, U.S.A. " "
104 North East Parlour, John Brown House, Providence, Rhode Island, U.S.A. " "
105 The Drawing-room, Rousham, Oxfordshire . . . . " "
106 The Staircase, Ragley Hall, Warwickshire . . . . " "
107 Hall and Staircase, 9 Henrietta Street, Dublin . . . " "
108 Upper storey of Staircase Hall, 15 Queen's Square, Bath . . " "
109 The Entrance Hall, Carter's Grove, Virginia, U.S.A. . . " "
110 Main Stairway, Benjamin Hall Junior House, Medford, U.S.A. . " "
111 Detail of Staircase, Battersea, Virginia, U.S.A. . . . " "
112 'Chinese' Staircase, Boughton House, Northamptonshire . . " "
113 The Stair Hall, second floor, Bohemia, Cecil County, Maryland, U.S.A. . " "
114 Chimney-piece in the Hall, Ragley Hall, Warwickshire . . " "
115 The Fire-place in the Library, Crichel House, Dorset . . " "
116 The Fire-place in the Front Room, 31 Old Burlington Street, London . " "
117 The Doorway in the Entrance Hall, Easton Neston, Northamptonshire . " "
118 A Door in the Tapestry Room, Hagley Hall, Worcestershire . . " "
119 A Door in the Gallery, Hagley Hall, Worcestershire . . " "
120, 121 Two Doorways in the Front Room, 31 Old Burlington Street, London " "
122 Carving in the Library, Ragley Hall, Warwickshire . . " "
123 Carved and gilt applied ornament in the Saloon, Marble Hall, Twickenham " "
124 Plaster ornamentation in the Drawing-room, Hagley Hall, Worcestershire " "
125 The Anteroom, Syon House, Isleworth . . . . " "
Staircase Ironwork from Welldon's *The Smith's Right Hand* . . *Page 53*
Fig. 126 The Long Gallery, Syon House, Isleworth . . . *Between pages 64 and 65*
127 The Hall, Harewood House, Yorkshire . . . . " "
128 The Ballroom, Lansdowne House, London . . . . " "
129 The Dining-room, Crichel House, Dorset . . . . " "
130 The Saloon, Boodle's Club, London . . . . " "
131 The Drawing-room, Crichel House, Dorset . . . . " "
132 The Drawing-room, Attingham House, Shropshire . . . " "
133 The Hall, Dodington Park, Gloucestershire . . . . " "
134 The Drawing-room, Dodington Park, Gloucestershire . . . " "
135 The Upper Landing, Dodington Park, Gloucestershire . . . " "
136 Providence House, Rhode Island, U.S.A. . . . . " "
137 The Library, Dodington Park, Gloucestershire . . . . " "
138 The Entrance Hall, Attingham House, Shropshire . . . " "
139 Detail of Ceiling, 17 St. Stephen's Square, Dublin . . " "
140 The Breakfast-room Ceiling, Harewood House, Yorkshire . . " "
141 Detail of the Dining-room Ceiling, Crichel House, Dorset . . " "
142 The Ceiling of the East Hall, Crichel House, Dorset . . " "
143 A section of the Dining-room Ceiling, Attingham, Shropshire . . " "
144 The Drawing-room Ceiling, Crichel House, Dorset . . . " "

xi

Fig. 145   Detail of the Dining-room Ceiling, Attingham House, Shropshire   *Between pages* 64 *and* 65

146   Ceiling of the Boudoir, Attingham House, Shropshire   ,,   ,,

147   Room on the ground floor, Dodington Park, Gloucestershire   ,,   ,,

148   The Stairway, Coleman-Hollister House, Greenfield, Massachusetts, U.S.A.   ,,   ,,

149   The Hall, Heveningham, Suffolk   ,,   ,,

150   The Etruscan Room, Osterley, Middlesex   ,,   ,,

151   The Print Room, Woodhall, Hertfordshire   ,,   ,,

152   The Gallery Ceiling, Harewood House, Yorkshire   ,,   ,,

153   The Committee Room Ceiling, Bank of England, London   ,,   ,,

154   The Hall, Dodington Park, Gloucestershire   ,,   ,,

155   The Staircase, Trinity House, Tower Hill, London   ,,   ,,

156   The Staircase Hall, Wentworth Woodhouse, Yorkshire   ,,   ,,

157   The East Hall, Crichel House, Dorset   ,,   ,,

158   The Arched Screen between the Hall and Staircase, Chicheley, Buckinghamshire   ,,   ,,

159   The first floor Staircase Hall, Crichel House, Dorset   ,,   ,,

160   The first floor Landing, Dodington Park, Gloucestershire   ,,   ,,

161   The Staircase, Harewood House, Yorkshire   ,,   ,,

162   The Entrance Hall, Dodington Park, Gloucestershire   ,,   ,,

163   Detail of the Painted Saloon, Heveningham, Suffolk   ,,   ,,

164   The Court Room, Bank of England, London   ,,   ,,

165   The Boudoir in the East Wing, Attingham, Shropshire   ,,   ,,

166   Doorway into the Small Hall, Crichel House, Dorset   ,,   ,,

167   The Small Drawing-room, Attingham, Shropshire   ,,   ,,

168   Detail of Wall and Chimney-piece at 4 Grafton Street, London   ,,   ,,

169   The Hall, Courteenhall, Northamptonshire   ,,   ,,

170   Chinese Wallpaper at Temple Newsam, Yorkshire   *Facing page* 73

       Classic Room, From Hope *Household Furniture*, 1807   *Page* 74

171   A Corridor in the Bank of England   *Between pages* 74 *and* 75

172   The Painted Parlour, Southill, Bedfordshire   ,,   ,,

173   The Dining-room, Southill, Bedfordshire   ,,   ,,

174   The Drawing-room, Crawley House, Bedfordshire   ,,   ,,

175   The Assembly Room, the Stamford Hotel, Stamford, Lincolnshire   ,,   ,,

176   The Back Parlour, Pitzhanger Manor, Ealing   ,,   ,,

177   The Library, Barnsley Park, Gloucestershire   ,,   ,,

178   The Staircase, Pelzer House, U.S.A.   ,,   ,,

179   The first floor Gallery, The Bedford Hotel, Brighton   ,,   ,,

180   The Entrance Hall, The Stamford Hotel, Stamford, Lincolnshire   ,,   ,,

181   The Library, Wimpole Hall, Cambridgeshire   ,,   ,,

182   Detail in the Dining-room, Southill, Bedfordshire   ,,   ,,

183   The Library, Barnsley Park, Gloucestershire   ,,   ,,

184   Wall-paper of Chinese type, of English manufacture   *Between pages* 76 *and* 77

185   The Banqueting Room, Brighton Pavilion   ,,   ,,

186   The Corridor, formerly the Chinese Gallery, Brighton Pavilion   ,,   ,,

187   The Music Room, Brighton Pavilion   ,,   ,,

188   The Dining-room, Eaton Hall, Cheshire   ,,   ,,

189   The Staircase, Eaton Hall, Cheshire   ,,   ,,

190   The Staircase, Strawberry Hill, Twickenham   ,,   ,,

191   The Gothic Library, Milton House, near Didcot, Berkshire   ,,   ,,

192   The Library, Arbury Hall, Warwickshire   ,,   ,,

193   The Staircase in the Entrance Hall, Ashridge House, Hertfordshire   ,,   ,,

194   The Library, Strawberry Hill, Twickenham   ,,   ,,

195   The Library, Eaton Hall, Cheshire   ,,   ,,

DECORATION OF THE EARLY RENAISSANCE (1500-1650)

Introduction: The Interior

The Italian Influence under Henry VIII—The Elizabethan Agricultural and Trading Expansion—The Early Seventeenth-century Building Period—The Reign of Charles I—The Commonwealth

THE sixteenth century and the Tudor dynasty coincided with a period of rapid growth and change. The magnificence of English courtly surroundings in the reign of Henry VIII, who built or added to New Hall, Nonsuch, Bridewell, and St. James's, impressed foreign visitors. and the Papal legate, Chiergati, wrote that 'the wealth and civilization of the world are here'. Henry VIII was the first English king to form a collection of pictures, which hung in the gallery in Whitehall. He was 'the onlie phoenix of his time for fine and curious masonrie,' and attracted foreign artists to his Court and service. The King's advisers were by 1545 alarmed at this foreign influx, and Paget roundly blamed Lord Cobham for his 'having been the occasion of the coming of so many with which all here are wearied'. 'My lord' (the postscript runs), 'I beseech you send over no more strangers, and move the rest there to send none, for the king is not content'.[1]

The first beginnings of a study of Italian art and architecture date from Henry's reign. John Shute, whose patron was the Duke of Northumberland, visited Italy for that purpose, and on his return published the first work in English on Renaissance architecture, *The Chief Groundes of Architecture* (1563). The Renaissance was not completely assimilated in England; in ornament, its alphabet was substituted for the Gothic, but there are survivals of late Gothic detail.

The King's example was followed by his favourites, the 'new men', described as 'scant well-born gentlemen of no great lands till they were promoted by us', such as Henry Lord Marney, the builder of Layer Marney Tower; Sir Richard Weston, the builder of Sutton Place; Lord Sandys, the builder of the Vyne; and men of the commonalty, such as Wolsey, for nearly twenty years *de facto* ruler of England, who spent his immense revenues in building. The state of Wolsey's palaces, the richness of his household stuff, his arras stiff with gold, his oriental carpets and gold and silver plate were a marvel to chroniclers and an offence to his enemies. At his death the 'onlie phoenix' in building had exhausted his treasury, and left a legacy of debt to his successor. The youth of the new King and the brevity of the reign of Mary left no time for Royal patronage.

With the long reign of Elizabeth, architecture and decoration had passed into a new phase. In this reign, prices rose with the increase of industrial and trading activity; the landowners prospered, and it was not unusual for gentlemen landowners to make profit out of their estates, 'turning farmers and graziers for money.' Whereas at the beginning of the sixteenth century, the tenant farmers rarely had more than a few shillings of ready money, at its close, despite the increased rents, they were able to put by considerable sums. This reign saw the rise of the families based on sheep farming, and of the great country house, built to express and display this new wealth. Wollaton Hall was, it was said, built by Sir Francis Willoughby 'for a foolish display of his wealth.' Hardwick Hall and Burghley are expressive of their builders. The builders did, in the full sense of Harrison's words, 'dailie imagine new devises to guide their workmen withall'[2] they set their initials on the balustrade, recorded their arms and alliances

[1] R. W. Carden, *Proc. Soc. Ant.*, 28th March, 1912.　　　　[2] Harrison, *Description of England*, p. 318.

on the stuccoed ceiling, on the chimney-piece, and in the windows, and saw to every detail of the plan, the finishing, and furnishing. This widespread use of armorial bearings was denounced by Stubbes as a capital instance of the vice of pride. 'Every one,' he says, 'vaunts himself, crying with open mouth, "I am gentleman, I am worshipful, I am honourable, I am noble, and I cannot tell what; my father was this, my father was that; I am come of this house, and I am come of that." '[1] Houses of the late sixteenth and early seventeenth century were large, for a gentleman's house might have to be the sovereign's for a few days when on her progresses, and she imposed upon them an endeavour to exhibit their loyalty in costly entertainments. Throughout this age (until the closing of the theatres in 1642) masque and pageantry held their place in the public eye and in the public interest, and in these the strange medley of past and present, sacred and profane only reflected the medley present in men's minds. 'Pedantry, novelty, the allegory of Italy, the mythology of Rome, the English bear-fight, pastorals, superstition, farce', all took their turn in the entertainment which Lord Leicester provided for the Queen at Kenilworth. Many interiors are pageants in woodwork, plaster, and stone, which were influenced by the contemporary love for spectacles in which the learning, the craftsmanship, and imagination of the age were expended in the production of so much transitory magnificence.

The extension of trade, as London grew into the general market of Europe, and the establishment of Gresham's Royal Exchange, mark the country's commercial progress. The silver from the Mexican and Peruvian mines, and also the development of the African trade led to an immense increase in the supply of precious metals, of which quantities were used for plate, and it has been computed that one-fifth of the supply was used in this manner in England during the sixteenth and seventeenth centuries,[2] when even men of the middle class had their garnish of silver. The formation of capital for trading ventures and industry was rendered easier by the supply of silver in circulation. Wealth was created by the new trading ventures of the late sixteenth and early seventeenth century, when the granting of charters to the Eastland (Baltic) Company (1579), to the Levant Company (1581), to the Guinea Company (1588), and the foundation of the Great East India Company (1600)—witnesses to the Elizabethan spirit of enterprise.

The first forty years of the seventeenth century formed a great building period. 'No kingdom in the world spent so much in building'[3] as England did in James I's reign. The largest of the great houses of the early Renaissance, such as Audley End and Blickling, date from this reign. Houses for the merchant adventurers, who, not content with ancient trade-routes, were sending vessels to the East and West Indies, to the Canaries, even to China, Muscovy, and Tartary, rose in London and the greater provincial towns. The full inventory of the household stuff of the Earl of Northampton, taken in 1614, reveals a number of curiosities from the East, together with carpets, porcelain, and rich silks. The wealth of the great merchants of London and the other chief ports can be gauged by the contemporary complaints of the extravagance in housekeeping and dress of this class.[4] The plan of the house followed traditional lines after fashion had adopted foreign decoration. 'The one quality which the Italian influence gradually introduced into the plan was symmetry, and this could be obtained without sacrificing the arrangements which seemed essential to English habits'.[5] No definite ratio between the height, width and length of rooms was aimed at and the plan was often irregular; in the great chamber at South Wraxall, a mass of masonry required to carry the roofs projects boldly into the room and is emphasized as a decorative feature. The early Tudor interiors that have survived, such as the Abbot's lodging at Thame Park, have a restraint in contrast with the lavishness of the succeeding period, when the designs by Low Countrymen and Germans giving illustrations of features such as doorways, interior porches, screens, and windows appealed to the surveyor, the carver, and the plasterer. Interiors were brilliantly coloured. A writer in 1558 remarks on the great use made in England of tapestry and

[1] *Anatomie of Abuses*, Part I (New Shakespeare Society's Publications) (1876), p. 29.   [2] W. Jacob, *An Historical Enquiry into the Production and Consumption of the Presious Metals*, vol. ii. p. 131.   [3] Dr G. Goodman, *The Court of James I* (1839), vol. i. p. 199.   [4] Though merchants still dressed soberly, their wives were said to show more extravagance in the adornment of their person than Court ladies.   [5] J. A. Gotch, *Early Renaissance Architecture in England*, London, 1913, p. 41.

painted cloths, and these, when fresh from the loom and the brush, formed a brilliant combination with the coloured and gilded plasterwork and carved ornament. The walls were either wainscoted, or hung with tapestry or stained cloth; the chimney-piece was as free an exercise in design as the contemporary marble and stone monuments in the church; the windows were coloured but not obscured by painted glass. In great houses there is no stint of good material, no end to the ardent prodigality of the craftsman, and the curiosity, excess, and variety in costume that troubled the satirist tricks out the interiors.

The sententiousness of the latter part of the sixteenth century, and a tendency to emphasize the national prosperity by allegorical figures of Peace and Plenty, is more marked in James I's reign. As in the contemporary emblem books, visible poetry and symbolism 'catching the eye and fancy at one draught' had an irresistible attraction. In the drawing-room at Bolsover, the Five Senses are painted on upper semicircular compartments of the walls. The hall at Burton Agnes, the state-room ceilings of Boston House are galleries of symbolism, in which the delight in ingenuity has run to excess; on the Burton Agnes screen alone the Twelve Tribes, the Sybils, Pax, Concordia, and the Four Evangelists are crowded together.

There was little differentiation of rooms. The hall was at first the arena of household life, where (as Aubrey,[1] writing in the later seventeenth century, remembered) the Lords of Manor, 'did eate at the high table or oreile, the folke at the side tables'. The feudal economy a thing of the past, the master of the house with his family withdrew to his 'parlour' and privacy. With the reduction of the large households and over-liberal housekeeping, the hall, though occupying a large space in the plan, became no more than a passage room, and in certain early seventeenth-century plans a separate dining-room is provided.[2] The description of the parlour of Hastings, a Dorset squire who died in 1650, must have had many parallels.[3] 'The corners of the room were full of the best chosen hunting and hawking poles; his oyster table at the lower end . . . was of constant use twice a day all the year round . . . ; the upper part of the room had two small tables and a desk, on the one side of which was a Church Bible, and on the other, *The Book of Martyrs*. On the tables were hawks' hoods, bells, and such like; . . . Tables, dice, cards, and boxes were not wanting.' The long gallery on the topmost floor, lighted from one side, is characteristic of the second half of the sixteenth and early seventeenth century. They were used for exercise and games, and as a promenade in wet and inclement weather. Sir Peter Legh of Lyme was often seated 'in the compas window of his gallerie,' hearing the claims and complaints of his tenants and paying his retainers' wages.[4] Here and in the hall were held the mummery and musical entertainments, and at Apethorpe there is evidence of its use as a music room. The long gallery must have been especially difficult to warm in the winter, and the fireplaces were supplemented by braziers that would be carried about the room as occasion required, and which at Knole still stand in the rooms where they were used.

The opening of the reign of Charles I does not mark a date in architectural design, and what may be termed 'Jacobean' methods are still dominant in Aston Hall, which was not completed until 1635. The appearance of the house was more compact but less picturesque; it was more regular, relying upon its proportions and its more scholarly detail. The style is of greater sobriety. Something is due to the influence of the King, and of the few travelled dilettanti, such as the Earl of Arundel. Charles was himself 'well-skilled in things of antiquity and could judge of medals, whether they had the number of years they pretended unto'. He was wont to say that 'he could get his living, if necessitated, by any trade he knew of, but the making of hangings'. He was an enlightened collector of works of art, and the inventory of his furniture, hangings, plate, pictures, and jewels took a year to complete. Lord Arundel, 'the Father of Vertu' in England, had acquired a knowledge of art in his travels in the Low Countries, France, and Spain. He formed the first large collection of works of art in this country, and from 1615 onwards he collected diligently, making purchases himself, and employing agents when he

[1] Aubrey, *North Wiltshire* (Topographical Collections), ed. Jackson (1862), p. 8. [2] *e.g.* Smithson's plan for Lord Sheffield's house (before 1626). [3] Ashley Cooper, Earl of Shaftesbury, *Fragment of Autobiography* (1859), pp. 22–25. [4] Lady Newton, *The House of Lyme*, p. 58.

was in England. The Venetian school of painting was the nucleus of his gallery, and the work of Holbein also specially appealed to him. Some of the marbles gathered by his agents in the Levant were arranged in a gallery shown in his portrait[1] as a high waggon-vaulted room with an arched opening and balcony in the Italian manner, and the gardens and galleries of Arundel House became a museum of ancient art. He was the 'first person of quality that brought in uniformity of building, and was the chief Commissioner to see it performed in London'. Peacham was gratified to observe the more intimate appreciation of the arts under the reign of Charles I, 'what a gentleman was expected to be acquainted with the great examples of sculpture and painting, and to draw a tasteful emblem'.[2] Even before Peacham, Richard Haydocke speaks of this new interest among the nobility and gentry 'as may appear by their galleries carefully furnished with the excellent monuments of sundry famous and ancient painters, both Italian and German';[3] and Webb was commissioned to purchase metals, statues, and works of art for the 'great nobility and eminent gentry'. The household gear pillaged from Claydon and Corfe Castle witnesses to an informed taste.

Sir Roger Pratt advises those about to build to rely upon some ingenious gentleman 'who hath seen much of that kind abroad, and been somewhat versed in the best authors of architecture, viz., Palladio, Scamozzi, Serlio', who would give them a design.

In Sir Henry Wotton's *The Elements of Architecture*, the ideals and standard of the travelled Englishman can be estimated and studied. All the Italian buildings which Wotton singles out for admiration, either in this book or in his letters, are the work of Palladio and Vignola, architects of the late Renaissance. To him beauty of proportion was the first object, and the duty of the architect 'to make the form, which is the noblest part, as it were triumph over the matter', and he writes of the 'graceful and harmonious contentment of the age' caused by rightly proportioned doors and windows.[4] '*The Elements of Architecture*, a collection of scattered notes and suggestions written not for an architect but for a gentleman of wealth intending to express himself in one of those great country palaces which were building, is of value as a summary of the attainement of the time,' and his brief study is an indication that architecture was dependent upon scholarship in design.

There was an increase of foreign travel among the propertied classes. Roger Pratt in 1643 visited France, Italy, Holland, and Flanders, 'to give himself some convenient education' in a tour lasting six years, which kept him away from England during the Civil War, and John Evelyn also 'absented himself from this ill face of things at home', travelling in France, the Low Countries, and Italy. Richard Boyle, first Earl of Burlington, was sent in his twentieth year to begin his travels into foreign kingdoms, his father allowing him a grant of a thousand pounds a year, and more than two years were spent by him in France, the Low Countries, and Italy; Sir William Temple began his travels in 1648, 'a time so dismall for England that none but they who were the occasion of those troubles and confusions in the country could be sorry to leave it':[5] to live in England at this time 'appeared worse than banishment'. In the Civil War the propertied classes were hard pressed. The cavaliers who had garrisoned their houses for the King suffered fines under the Commonwealth. Building was almost at a standstill; and beyond Coleshill (Fig. 36), begun at the close of this period, Lees Court in Kent (Fig. 32) and a certain amount of work by Webb, there is little new building between 1640 and the Restoration of monarchy. In the shock of Civil War, 'monies', (in the words of a contemporary letter), 'were not to be had for anything unless arms, swords, and muskets, which are gold and silver, plate and household stuff are not merchauntable'. There was widespread destruction of furniture and household stuff, especially after an obstinate siege; at Wardour Castle a chimney-piece valued at two thousand pounds was defaced, the parliamentarian troops hacking down all the carving with their pole-axes.

[1] Portrait (dated 1618) illustrated in Hervey, (M), *Life of Thomas Earl of Arundel*, Plate X.   [2] G. S. Gordon, Introduction to Peacham's *Compleat Gentleman*.   [3] Preface to *A tracte containing the Artes of curious Paintinge, Carvinge and Building, Oxford*, 1598 (translated from Lomazzo).   [4] *Reliquiæ Wottonianæ*, 4th edition, 1685, p. 34.   [5] *Works*, vol. i. p. iv.

Foreign Influences

The Italian Influence—The Influence of the Low Countries—The Jacobean Style—French and Italian Influences in the Reign of Charles I

TO the 'taste of the upper classes for foreign things alone,' which is animadverted on by Richard Mulcaster,[1] is due the foreign influences of the sixteenth century in England. During the reign of Henry VIII, the art of the Italian Renaissance was grafted into the native stock, and the history of English decoration from this time is the record of an imperfect but progressive assimilation. Many minor Italian artists and craftsmen figure in building accounts, and Italian artificers were admired in Tudor England as being 'the finest and most inventive workmen of all others.'[2] Of the immigrant Italians, Torregiano,[3] who was entrusted with the making of Henry VII's tomb, was the most celebrated; the contract for King Henry VII's tomb was made in 1512, and it was finished some time before 5th January, 1518–19. Another Italian, Benedetto da Rovezzano,[4] probably came to England before 1524 and contracted with Wolsey for a tomb, which was not to be inferior in workmanship or cost to that of King Henry VII. But Wolsey was not to lie beneath the tomb he had ordered. Toto del Nunziata,[5] who is believed to have been the chief decorative artist employed at Nonsuch, was nearly forty years resident in England, and Nicholas Bellin, called 'moulder' as well as 'paynter,' who had worked at Fontainebleau, was also for a considerable time in this country. Names of other Italians, Girolamo da Treviso,[6] Guido Mazzoni or Paganino, and others appear in the King's service, but their work has disappeared without a trace. Many of the lesser men were stuccoists, makers of decorative ornament, painters of heraldic designs, badges, and accessories for masques and pageants. The greatest of the immigrant artists was the South German, Hans Holbein, who came to England in 1526. It might have been expected that he, the master of all arts (*insignis artifex*, as Erasmus calls him), would have founded a school here. He had a practical knowledge of the various branches of the arts for which he supplied working drawings. He 'modelled and carved, was excellent in designing ornaments,' and invented patterns for goldsmiths' work, for enamelling and chasing of plate, arts much countenanced by Henry VIII. The surprising thing about this considerable immigration of foreigners is that it did not affect the architecture of England. Nonsuch was a Gothic fabric mounted with the Renaissance statues and bas-reliefs, and Italian detail was adopted, and the somewhat attenuated grace of Italian ornament blended with the general lines of Northern design. In the choir-stalls of Christchurch, Hampshire, dating from about 1528, the panels forming the back are headed at the top with eccentric Renaissance devices, and the medallioned heads are varied here and there by Gothic detail. Pure Renaissance detail appears on the tomb of Henry, Lord Marney, in Layer Marney Church, and the similar work at Oxburgh, on the Countess of Salisbury's chantry, Christchurch, and elsewhere in the south-eastern counties of England, especially in the neighbourhood of Winchester and of Southampton, a town which was the centre and port of Italian trade in England. The largest and most complete early Renaissance work in spirit and execution is the screen in the chapel of King's College, Cambridge, which must have been made between 1532 and 1536 from the presence of the initials and badge of Anne Boleyn, but there is unfortunately no record of its construction. With this exception, the extant early Renaissance ornament appears to be the work of some Italianate Low Countryman or Englishman rather than of an itinerant Italian. The ingredients of Italian ornament of the cinquecento

---

[1] *Positions*, p. 211. [2] W. Thomas, *The Histoire of Italie*, 1549. [3] Torregiano died in 1528. [4] Alfred Higgins, 'On the work of Florentine sculptors in England in the early part of the sixteenth century,' *Archaeological Journal*, September 1894, pp. 138–98. [5] Toto del Nunziata, a Florentine who was naturalized in 1538, was sergeant painter in 1543. He was still sergeant painter at the death of Edward VI. Bellin, who received a patent of denization in 1541, was engaged in 1551 on the completion of Henry VIII's tomb. [6] Girolamo da Treviso (1497–1544). According to Vasari he erected buildings in the Italian style which delighted and surprised the King beyond measure.

are there—the candelabra, the vases, the wreathed and medallioned heads, the foliage—but there is an odd incongruity in the northern treatment of the human figure; the 'nakyd chyldren'[1] of the accounts of the building of Hampton Court oddly translate the Italian *putti*. The medallioned heads vary from presentment of Roman emperors and oriental potentates (such as are frequently illustrated during the early Renaissance by continental engravers) to entirely fantastic personages grotesquely treated.

The Italian influence was partial and transient, depending, as it did, on the limited activity of a number of highly skilled craftsmen, and with the close of the first half of the century there is an end of detail of unmixed Italian origin. That succeeding influence from the Low Countries was longer-lived was to some extent due to the close religious and commercial ties between England and the Low Countries during the second half of the sixteenth and early seventeenth century; but to a greater extent to the importation of engravings and pattern books, furniture, monuments, and carved wainscot. Italy was far off and was not an exporting country; while the Low Countries, with the port of Antwerp as its fair and focus, was England's nearest and best market.

The Flemish immigration was already an offence to Londoners in Henry VIII's reign. The fire burst into flame in the evil May Day riots against the strangers and artificers who resided in the realm, to the great detriment of the English craftsmen, who could 'scarce get any living'. A certain John Lincoln, who led the disaffected Londoners, complained that 'the Dutchmen bring over iron, timber, leather, and wainscot ready wrought; nails, locks, baskets, cupboards, stools, tables, chests, and painted cloths, so that if they were wrought here Englishmen might get something by it'.[2] The rioters rose on 30th April 1517 and looted the houses of the stranger artificers. The uprising was unsuccessful, and Low Country immigrants and goods continued to pour into England by way of Antwerp. Guicciardini gives a valuable account of the extent and value of our trade with Antwerp in 1568. To England Antwerp exported jewels, wrought silks, tapestry, glass, small wares made of metal, and household furniture, among other commodities, and the annual importation into Antwerp about this date amounted to more than 200,000 pieces, a sum which was invested in Low Country goods adapted for the English market. The correspondence of Sir Thomas Gresham and his agent, Richard Clough, shows to what extent English buildings were indebted to the Low Countries in the matter of design, decoration, and materials. Sir Thomas employed a Fleming, Henryk, for the building of the Burse, or Royal Exchange,[3] and all the materials, down to the statue of Queen Elizabeth and the paving stones, were shipped from Antwerp under his direction. The Royal Exchange was not the only building the Flemish master workman had a hand in, for Gresham[4] lent him to Cecil in the latter part of 1567. Richard Clough, who had lived in Flanders, built his small house, Bachegraig,[5] in Denbighshire, in the Flemish style, and of Flemish materials.

The decoration of the great English houses was often finished off by Low Countrymen like Henryk, who would submit patterns, 'platts', and models for a bay window, a chimney-piece or a porch, and the execution of the carved detail was often given to the more highly skilled Low Countryman. For the wainscoting of the hall[6] of Queen's College, Cambridge, in 1531, two or three carpenters were employed, the arms of benefactors and medallioned heads being executed by Giles Fambeler and Dyrik Harrison, names which have a foreign sound. At Hatfield[7] the joiners' work, wainscoting, and designing of the chimney-pieces were given to one Jenever, a 'Dutchman', living in London, while Hoocker, of St Martin's Lane, who made the turners' work, was probably of the same nationality.[8]

---

[1] November 1535. 'In the Kynges long gallery Ende a border of antyke wyth nakyd chyldren, the antyke all gylte, the fyld layde with fybe byse', quoted in E. Law, *Hampton Court*, vol. i. p. 365. [2] Hall, *The triumphant reigne of Kynge Henry the VIII* (ed. Whibley), 1904, vol. i. p. 156. [3] The foundation of the Royal Exchange was laid on 7th June 1566. [4] Burgon, *Life and Times of Sir Thomas Gresham*, 1839, vol. ii. p. 503. [5] Bachegraig is illustrated in the *Life and Times of Sir Thomas Gresham*, vol. ii. Plate II. The roof is pagoda-shaped and Flemish in character. In a Welsh elegiac poem we read:—   'At Bachegraig he reared a stately pile
                                   Of strong materials, which he brought from Antwerp,
                                   Thence, too, his mansion's marble pillars came.'
[6] Willis and Clark, *Architectural History of Cambridge*, Cambridge, 1888, vol. ii. pp. 44–45, and Appendix, p. 61. [7] Completed in 1611. [8] *Victoria County History of Hertfordshire*, London, 1912, vol. iii, p. 96, S.P. Dom., James I, vol. xiii. No. 88 (1).

Bernard Jansen or Janssen, stone-mason and tombmaker,[1] was employed at Audley End. A certain Giles de Witt,[2] 'marbeller', was at work at Cobham in 1594, and the porch and marble chimney-piece in the picture gallery[3] show their Flemish origin.

Woodwork and weaving were the most common occupations of these immigrants. In an epitome of the returns of the city companies in 1583, one hundred joiners and seventy-three weavers head the list of occupations.[4] Besides these humble craftsmen a group of Low Country artists, sculptors, and painters in London worked together in the late sixteenth and early seventeenth century. Maximilian Coult or Colt,[5] a sculptor from Arras, settled in England at the close of Elizabeth's reign and was appointed master carver to the King in 1628. In 1633 he had the post of Master Sculptor to the King. The two Cuers or Cures, father and son, were also sculptors and marble-masons; the elder,[6] Cornelius (who was of Dutch origin), master mason to Queen Elizabeth, was employed in the monuments to Mary, Queen of Scots, and Elizabeth, while his son, William Cure, succeeded him as master mason to James I, and completed the monument to Mary, Queen of Scots. The marble-mason was the purveyor of marble chimney-pieces of which examples closely similar in design are found in great houses of the early seventeenth century, such as Knole (Fig. 4), Bramshill, Hatfield, and Charlton. The fact that Cornelius Cuer[7] was paid for stones for the chimney-piece in the drawing chamber at Knole, indicates the Low Country origin of these designs in which panelling of contrasting marbles were employed.

A later designer of monuments, Nicholas Stone,[8] though of English birth (he was the son of a Devon quarryman) was closely connected with Holland by training. About the time of James I's accession, he entered the workshop of Henrik de Keyser, a monumental mason of Amsterdam, whose daughter he married and with whom he had close business ties. Though he did a certain amount of work as an architect it is chiefly by his monuments that he is now best known. Stone's work is always interesting and individual, influenced by his Dutch apprenticeship; as master-mason—he was appointed master-mason and architect in 1626—he supplied chimney pieces for Kirby Hall and other English houses. The Civil War broke in upon Stone's activities, and the items in his note-book are very meagre after 1641.[9] These are cases where there is documentary evidence of Low Country influence; in other cases, as in the chimney-pieces in the library at Rothamsted, though there is no direct evidence of Flemish handiwork, there is a strong presumption of it from the character of the work and the Flemish connexions of the Witterwronges.[10] The designs of Flemish and German pattern books by Bluom,[11] Dietterlein, and De Vries[12] were freely used. These engravings by De Vries published at Antwerp usually bear no date, but as de Vries resided at Antwerp from 1563 to 1570, and again from 1575 to 1585, it is probable that his books of design date from his connexion with Antwerp, and would be accessible to English craftsmen during the great building period of the late sixteenth and early seventeenth century. His *Architectura*, published in 1577, marks the beginning of the phase of Low Country design in England, first observable in Wollaton House (built in 1580), and dominant later in the early seventeenth-century houses, such as Audley End and Charlton House. The simplification by Smithson of de Vries's designs is characteristic of the English temper. It is significant that the houses that are Flemish in decoration are situated in the south-eastern counties and in easy reach of London, the centre of the foreign colony. The designs of the Utrecht firm of Crispin van de Passe (at the head of which is the elder Crispin),[13] was represented in London by Simon and Willem de Passe, the former between

[1] Fl. 1610–1630. [2] His names as a 'Dutchman, born at Bridges in Flanders, marbeller', appears among the 'strangers forreiners abiding in London, April–May 1593'. Kird, 'Records of Aliens in London', *Proc. Soc. Huguenot* (1907), p. 445. [3] Dated 1599. [4] Kirk, 'Returns of Aliens' (1571–97), *Proc. Soc. Huguenot*, 1902, Preface. [5] Colt's name was originally Poultrain, and in early life he is often destribed as Powtran or Poutraine, *alias* Colt. Colt is met with as late as 1641, when he was imprisoned in the Fleet. His nephew John Coult (Colte) also a sculptor, petitioned to succeed Maximilian. [6] D. 1607. [7] Jackson, *The Renaissance of Roman Architecture*, p. 122. [8] B. 1587. [9] A. E. Bullock, *Some Sculptural Works of Nicholas Stone*, A.D. 1596–1647, London, 1908. [10] The house was bought in 1623 by the widow of a refugee from Ghent, Jacques Witterwronghele. [11] Bluom's work, published at Zurich in 1550, is declared on the title-page to be useful to painters, sculptors, workers in brass or wood, masons and statuaries. It was translated into English in 1608. [12] Jan Vredeman de Vries, 1527–1608. [13] The elder Crispin van de Passe had worked in Cologne, whither he had migrated not later than 1594. By 1612 he was settled in Utrecht, and remained there until his death in 1637.

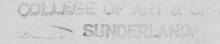

1616 and 1621, the latter filling his place after 1621 and remaining in London until his death in 1637. At Antwerp, then the commercial centre of Western Europe, 'the number of patient and more or less skilful hands employed between 1560 and 1640 in cutting images on plates of copper for the rolling press passes belief.' . . . Maps, illustrations to books of history, topography and travel, allegorical and emblematic frontispieces and title-pages of books, decorative borders or compartments enclosing subjects of history and myth, patterns for the sculptor, joiner, and architect poured without stint from these ateliers. The dependence of the craftsman upon pattern books can be gauged by comparing the ornament at Charlton House in Kent with Abraham de Bruyn's panels of figures and animals in grotesque ornament round a central cartouche containing a mythological scene. An oval medallion entitled Medusa figures in the upper stage of the chimney-piece in the white drawing-room; a medallion of Danaë in the south-east bedroom. The ornament surrounding the oval medallion of the sacrifice of Isaac, in the upper stage of the chimney-piece in the state drawing-room at Boston House, Brentford (Fig. 29), is taken from Abraham de Bruyn's panel entitled Andromeda in the same series, reproduced on page 9. Details of the ornament surrounding the medallion of Danae in the south-east bedroom at Charlton are borrowed from the same series.

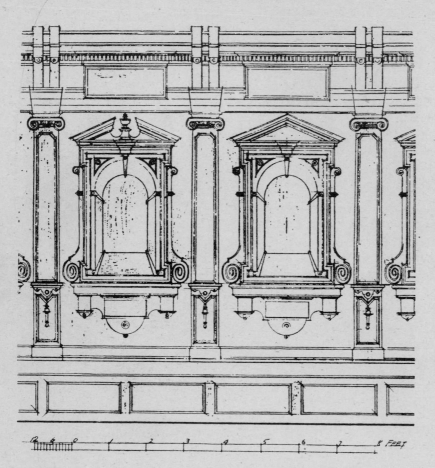

Panelling of the Stall Backs, the Convocation House, Oxford.
J. Gillespie del.

It is natural that, based as this detail is upon de Bruyn, its relative refinement and expertise should have been commented on: 'The primitive views on anatomy, and the barbarous treatment common to so much carved work of the Elizabethan and Jacobean periods are not altogether lacking in these mantelpieces, but they are more thoughtful in design and expert in handling' than in many other examples.[1] The Renaissance was elaborated by the Flemings in their own way. As in art they were unable to make a large, free gesture in design, but contented themselves with the fabric of complex detail, so in the details of architecture and decoration they specialized in strapwork, enlivened with small grotesques, in minute surface enrichment, in eccentricity of outline in features such as terminal caryatides, and in the representation in paint of Italian marbles.

Elizabethan work is (like the Elizabethans themselves) turbulent and energetic. The orders, used in the crudest fashion and seen through the medium of Flemish pattern books, are a frequent feature of interior decoration, and with them grotesque terminal caryatides and strapwork. 'Regular columns',

[1] *Country Life*, 8th May 1909.

as Walpole writes, 'with ornaments neither Grecian nor Gothic, and half embroidered with foliage, were crammed over frontispieces, façades, and chimneys, and lost all grace by wanting simplicity'.[1] Audley End struck an Italian visitor in Charles II's reign not as classic building, but as inclining 'to the Gothic, mixed with a little of the Doric and Ionic'.[2] Pillars were placed on pedestals, and the orders were assimilated in character, the Doric being in many cases as decorated as the Corinthian. The shafts were enriched with surface carving or broken by faceted or sculptured bands until the reign of Charles I.

In the reign of Charles I, allied by marriage with France, there is evidence of two French architects practising in England, Solomon[3] and Isaac de Caux; and Barbet's designs for chimney-pieces were laid under contribution by Inigo Jones. (Figs. 33–35). The presence in England of the French sculptor, Hubert le Sueur, 'his majesty's servant', the 'best statuary that ever this country enjoyed',[4] and of an Italian Francesco Fanelli (who describes himself as 'Scultore de Re della Gran Bretagne'), witness to the bias towards the art of

Panel of grotesque ornament, with centre medallion of Andromeda. The grotesque ornament is used in the chimney-piece at Boston House, Brentford, (Fig. 29.) *From an engraving by Abraham de Bruyn.*

France and Italy, and there are Italian features, pergolas, grates, Italian windows and doors, in the designs of Smithson. But this new development of English art was checked by the outbreak of civil war.

Decorative Painting and Colouring

Wall Paintings—Early Printed Papers—Colour—Paper Hangings

ALTHOUGH many rooms in the early Renaissance were wainscoted or hung with tapestries for warmth, others were decorated with wall paintings upon plaster. The general use of wainscot (and still later, of wall-paper) suppressed or overlaid such decorations which, as a rule, only come to light during alterations or restorations, and have been in many cases destroyed by workmen before they could be recorded and figured. They are painted both in black or colours, in oil

[1] *Anecdotes of Painting in England* (ed. Wornum), vol. i. p. 128.   [2] Magalotti, *Travels of Cosmo, Grand Duke of Tuscany* (in 1669), 1821, p. 204. [3] Solomon de Caux was at work at Wilton, and was paid in 1612 for works done at Greenwich and Somerset Gardens. Walpole, *Anecdotes of Painting in England* (ed. Wornum), vol. 1. p. 233, note.   [4] He supplied the statues of Charles I and Henrietta Maria at St John's College, Oxford.

colours in a rapid brush work, often without the use of stencils. The extent to which such painting was practised is shown by the considerable remains which have been discovered at Rothamsted where, besides a painting in the dining-room, there are traces of mural design at the dais end, and painted newels on the wall of the staircase hall.[1] The designs range from simple repeating devices to heraldic and ornamental compositions and figure subjects, often both crude in design and summary in execution. The collection of designs shown in the Saffron Walden Museum (which were mainly obtained in the immediate neighbourhood) is also evidence of the wide prevalence of this colour decoration in houses of the fifteenth, sixteenth, and early seventeenth centuries in the eastern counties (page 11).

An example of simple black-and-white designs, partaking of the character of Italian cut velvets, is preserved in the Priest's House, West Hoathly. The design consists of a series of octagons, within which are polygonal compartments filled with sprays of roses and vines. There existed three rooms decorated in black and white in a small one-storeyed house known as Campions, in the parish of Saffron Walden. In two rooms in which the designs were almost identical, the oak studs were painted black, and down each compartment enclosed by the studs bold black zigzags were painted forming triangular compartments, enclosing a formal design. In an upper room in the same house a brilliant design in eight colours has been preserved. It represents a semicircular-headed arcade of spirally-twisted columns outlined in black and white, in which the panels are filled in by a conventional design representing a curtain or tapestry, hanging from the arches. Above the arcading is a horizontal frieze of flowers and foliage[2] painted on a light purple ground, while on a panel above is inscribed in black letters 'Gyve to the pore, Spend and be b(lest)'. In a house at Royston coloured distemper decoration was found in opening out the upper part of a closed staircase. Here the wall surface is divided into panels executed in stencil and by hand. The stencilled panels are in chrome colour, with an indian red background, and the borders on each side of these panels dividing them from the panels executed by hand are in indian red. These panels show a vertical design of fruit, birds, and an armless terminal figure.[3] The royal arms and animals were often represented. In a house in Market Street, Rye, the mural painting consists of a frieze with the royal arms and cartouches bearing texts from the Bible, while beneath there is a flowing design in which is represented an elephant, a stag, a hound, a fox, a swan, and various birds.[4] The mural paintings discovered behind wainscot at Rothamsted appear to be of the latter half of the sixteenth century.[5] In the dining-room, the upper portion of the decoration represents a battle scene, while the lower is painted with Renaissance columns. In shell-headed niches between these is represented an animal. This example is yellowish-brown shaded with black and relieved with white lights, giving a marble effect.

In the frieze from the great chamber at Gilling (Fig. 2) the design consists of a formal tree, hung with the shields of the dwellers in each Wapentake of Yorkshire whom the visitation in 1584 recognized as entitled to coat armour. As there are not enough Wapentakes to go round, there is in the intervening space a painting of a party sitting on benches backed by a *treillage* of briars and vines. Figure subjects are an interesting class; at Pittleworth Manor in Hampshire there was discovered on the walls of an upper room a complete painted decoration of two dates. In the centre of one wall are the royal arms,[6] and to the left of these Dives, seated at table among a company dressed in costumes indicating luxury and extravagance, while (to the right of the royal arms) Dives is shown about to strike Lazarus. The wall to the left of the entrance door is painted with a rich pomegranate-patterned textile, which is carried over the oak studs, giving the appearance of hanging folds.[7] At Grove House, which stood close to Woodford Common until 1832, the paintings (described in the *Gentleman's Magazine*)[8] represented twelve scenes of country pleasures and occupations, and of these six were still fairly perfect.

1 'Some Mural Paintings at Rothamsted', by V. T. Hodgson, *St Albans and Herts. Architectural and Archæological Society*, vol. i. (N.S.), 1895–1902, p. 378.   2 Miller Christy and Guy Maynard, *Early Domestic Decorative Wall Paintings recently Discovered in Essex*. (Reprinted from the *Essex Archæological Society*, 1911, pp. 26–31.)   3 *St Albans and Herts. Architectural and Archæological Society* (N.S.), 1895, vol. i. p. 368.   4 *Coll. Sussex Archæological Society*, vol. i. pp. 117–24 (1904).   5 *St Albans Architectural and Archæological Society Trans.* (N.S.), vol. i. (1895–1902), p. 378. 6 Dated 1580.   7 The black-letter inscription gives full details of 'Dives and poore Lazarus the Scripture'.   8 *Gentleman's Magazine*, col. ciii. (Part II), 1833, pp. 393–95.

One, which was illustrated, represented a party of guests on a lawn of a moated house, seated at table, drinking, singing, and playing musical instruments. The painting bore the monogram $^D_M{}^C$ and the date 1617. On the southern wall of the great hall of the Carpenters' Company the compartments between the corbels which supported the original timber roof are filled in with arabesque work, enlivened with monsters, cupids, and cornucopiæ, and ornamental panels and foliations in a very decayed and imperfect condition. The author of these was no doubt Baker the painter, who was paid in 1571 for making the 'story in the parlour'.[1]

1. From Seward's End, Saffron Walden.   2, 3. From the Gabriel Hervey House.

1, 2, 3. Local Wall paintings in the Saffron Walden Museum.

In a recently[2] discovered decoration at the White Swan Hotel, Stratford on Avon, the paintings executed between about 1553 and 1565 were found by the shifting of some panelling. The painting is limited to the north wall of a ground-floor room, which is decorated with the Apocryphal story of Tobit, with explanatory inscriptions in block letter in the frieze above, and the odd spaces are filled in with fruit and foliage in green, shaded and outlined in white (Figs. 21–23). A series has also been discovered in an Elizabethan Manor House in Worcestershire, Harvington Hall.[3] Here numerous wall paintings were being uncovered from under several coats of whitewash. The greater part of the work is Elizabethan. Some of the finest draughtsmanship is on the second-floor landing, where the remains of six pictures have been found, probably part of a series of paintings of the Nine Worthies, though only one (a drawing of David slaying Goliath) can be identified as one of the accepted nine. On the walls of the staircase and adjoining passages are arabesques in black and white, with occasional human figures coloured pink. An ambitious scheme of decoration, removed from Hill Hall, Essex, consisted of a series of panels painted with scenes from the story of Cupid and Psyche after engravings from

[1] E. Jupp, *History of Carpenters' Company* (1887), pp. 226 and 235; and *Records of the Carpenters' Company* (1916), vol. iv. (1546–71) p. 144 (ed. B. Marsh).   [2] In 1927.   [3] The rebuilding of the hall dates from the ownership of John Pakington (who died in 1578).

Raphael by the 'Master of the Die', and these are far removed from the average level of Elizabethan painters.[1] The walls of a room on the first floor were covered about 1530 with a series of paintings in black and white, consisting of Renaissance ornament including enriched pilasters, arabesque, and *putti*. At the close of the sixteenth century, the walls were wainscoted to a height of about six and a half feet, and the space above painted with a second series of floral design, making a wide frieze. The date of this second series can be fixed between 1560 and 1581.

A wall painting dated 1603 was found at Paramour Grange, near Sandwich, in Kent, where canvas stretched upon battens protected the decoration. On the frieze round the room, broken by small panels containing a Tudor rose, a portcullis, a crown and a fleur-de-lys, are the Beatitudes in black-letter, beneath which is a line of bead and reel in black and white. 'Below again, the decoration depends upon a large strapwork hexagon, with a central square, all in black, making a simple and effective repeat. In each square is a coloured flower, and in the other spaces of the hexagon two unrecognizable fruits are placed, painted with a reddish and greenish colour alternating'.[2] By the same hand is the grisaille painting[3] on plaster from an old house at Stodmarsh in West Kent, representing emblems of the planets Jupiter, Venus, and Mercury, with signs of the zodiac and the months, which is especially interesting as an instance of the use of the engraved designs of the German Vergil Solis. From the same house is taken the grisaille painting of the story of Diana and Actæon in the same collection. Mural paintings of the type described do not appear to be later in date than the reign of James I. In the decoration of the walls and roof of two attics in the Meeting House, West Hanningfield, Essex, the panels are painted in brown, black, and white with large foliated and interlacing designs, in which centaurs, fishes, and terminal creatures figure, bordered with a narrower scroll design. In one panel is the date 1615, and a shield of Skynner impaling Folkes or Folke and Bowyer.

As the seventeenth century advanced, more ambitious decorative painting was attempted, perhaps by the foreign painters resident in London, who had to pay fines for following their art without being free of the Painter-Stainers' Company. Vaughan the Silurist heads a poem with the explanation that it was written 'upon a meeting with some of his friends at the Globe Tavern in a chamber painted overhead with a cloudy sky and some few dispersed stars, and on the sides with landscapes, hills, shepherds, and sheep'.

COLOUR

The use of colour for the enrichment of wainscoted walls and modelled plaster ceilings was a feature of Tudor and early Stuart interiors, and the effect of intricate brilliance and importance aimed at was obtained by tinting architectural members and picking out ornamental details. A coloured drawing by C. J. Richardson of the interior porch at Montacute, in which the ground of the woodwork is left its natural colour, while the carved enrichments are picked out in clear colour—red, blue, and yellow—vividly represents the original magnificence of Elizabethan decoration. Interiors of the Tudor period glowed with primary colours and gold. Cavendish makes reference to Wolsey's roof of 'gold and byse' (light blue) at Hampton Court, which seems to have been a favourite combination. In a contemporary account of Theobald's the ceilings are described as blue, with roses and other ornaments gilded;[4] and traces of red-blue, and yellow could be seen until recently on the plaster at Boughton Malherbe, in Kent. Painted decoration in imitation of intarsia or inlay, dated 1599, survives in Queen Mary's room at Hardwick Hall, Derbyshire, the scroll designs being painted in black. The Kederminster Library, built by Sir John Kederminster in 1617, in Langley Church, is the most complete and untouched survival of seventeenth-century colour decoration. The larger horizontal panels, which are

---

[1] Some fragments of these are now in the Victoria and Albert Museum, see article, *Burlington Magazine*, March 1941.   [2] Note to coloured drawings of the room.   [3] W. 24, 1913, Victoria and Albert Museum.   [4] Quoted in W. B. Rye, *England as Seen by Foreigners* (1865), p. 45.

painted with elaborate cartouches, are varied with narrow upright panels in which saints are represented; and the chimney-piece is also painted with arabesques, symbolical figures, and shields of arms on the convex centre of the upper stage (Figs. 11, 12). There are traces of early seventeenth-century colour decoration at Bramshill; in the flower-de-luce room the pattern is of a golden-coloured fleur-de-lys on dark green ovals, which occur in the centre of each panel. In the white rooms were traces, before they were repainted, of arabesque patterns in dark green, blue and black on the white panels.[1] The colouring of wainscot continued until the Restoration and in an inventory of Wimbledon Hall (taken in 1649) the oak wainscot was varnished green spotted with gold stars and crosses, or coloured 'livor colour' and varnished, or white, filleted with green.[2]

The use of several colours combined lost ground in the course of the seventeenth century, and woodwork was painted white or left in its natural colour, though ornamental details were occasionally gilded. The crest room from Albyns is painted white, with charges from the Abdy arms painted in the centre of each panel; and at Holland House, the white parlour was painted white with gilt enrichments.

PAPER HANGINGS

The beginnings of paper-hanging start in the sixteenth century, when stamped papers were made to line chests or boxes; and a few of these have been found fixed to the walls, or on to the panels into which the surface was divided. Such survivals have been accidentally preserved behind a later panelling, or have been removed from the interior of old boxes and drawers. The earliest known survival is the block-printed paper dating from the reign of Henry VIII, discovered during alterations at the Master's Lodge, Christ's College, Cambridge. This design centring in a large pomegranate with a charged centre and surrounding foliatials, closely follows North Italian velvets of contemporary date. A sheet of wall paper with a pattern of oval panels containing the arms of England, repeated, surrounded by panels filled with vases of fruit, or Tudor roses, was found on the walls of an old house at Besford.[3] In these instances, the paper was found upon walls, but it is impossible to say whether a number of early printed papers found as lining papers also served as wall coverings. One of the finest and most simple decorations has been recently discovered in the Golden Cross Inn at Oxford.

Woodwork

Clinker-boarding—Early Tudor Panelling—Linenfold—Medallioned Heads—Late Tudor Panelling—The Orders —Jacobean Wainscot—Construction—Carving—Woods

ENGLISH craftsmen, trained as they were in the Middle Ages in the building of timber-framed houses and the framing of timber roofs for churches and halls, turned readily to working in wood, and found full scope in the oak wainscot whereby rooms were 'made warme and more close than otherwise they would be'.[4]

The earliest wainscot recorded appears to have been plain boards, fixed side by side and painted; and there exist rare examples of narrow overlapping boards, or 'clinker-boarding', nailed to the wall, as in the porch of the Guildhall at Lavenham. Framed panelling is distinct from this earlier arrangement, and consists of a framework of uprights and cross-pieces enclosing long panels, which were

[1] Sir W. Cope, *The History of Bramshill*, pp. 52–53. [2] *Archæologia*, vol. x. pp. 401, 402, 403, 404. [3] Now in the Victoria and Albert Museum, E. 3593—1913. [4] Harrison, in Holinshed (ed. 1807), vol. i. p. 315.

enriched with cusping or with painting. The length of wainscot panels was reduced in the early Renaissance, and the panel became an oblong of which the height is not much greater than its width. In the early sixteenth century the panel was ornamented with various devices, of which the best known is the linen pattern, or linenfold, so called from the ornament resembling (at any rate, in certain examples) a piece of material arranged in vertical folds upon it. There is no reason to suppose that the

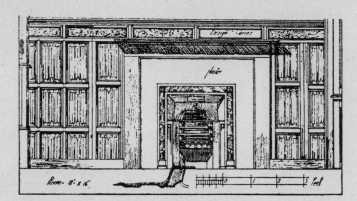

Side of a wainscoted room, formerly in the Old Neptune Inn, Ipswich.

device in its original form was derived from folded drapery. The linenfold does not appear in manuscripts earlier than the middle of the fifteenth century, and is first represented with a single rib dividing off the ornament into two folds.[1] In certain examples, the folded drapery is given an incised or relieved border, based on the selvedge or borders of the woven fabrics of the period; and, on one example, buttons and cords are carved for its suspension. In certain cases the rods upon which the drapery is rolled project beyond the edges, and are ornamented with spiral twists or foliations, and the edges of these folds are indented and cut back into fantastic hollows.

The pattern, which appears first in the northern districts of France, was in use before the sixteenth century in England.[2] Among examples that can be dated approximately by emblems and badges is the panelling at the Vyne, dating from between 1520–1525,[3] which is crisply carved with folds rolled on spirally-twisted foliated rods, and with royal badges, (such as pomegranates and fleurs-de-lys), shields, roses, short mottoes, cardinals' hats; linked initials filling in the spaces where the linenfold is cut back. Linenfold panelling was made for the hall of Queen's College, Cambridge,[4] in 1531, in which the panels were surmounted by a frieze containing the arms of benefactors alternating with heads richly carved.

Linenfold panels made about 1520 for the house of Coo, a rich Norwich merchant in Dial Yard, are remarkable for their finish and refined design, which equals any contemporary continental woodwork. The most important are the seven panels originally set over the chimney-piece, in which the owner's name, a shield bearing his merchant's mark, and the arms of the Mercers' Company appear in the cut-out spaces. The edges of the folds are cusped; and the rod foliated and elaborated at the upper and slipped at the lower extremity.

Medallioned heads, a *motif* of the Italian Renaissance, appear in certain panels. These, which are usually in profile, wear foliated helmets or eccentric caps and head-dress. Panels containing heads within a wreath with panels filled with ornament of Italian character appear in some of the early

---

[1] *e.g.* In an illustration in *Horae B. Mar. Virginis*, which contains an autograph of Henry VII, *B.M., Add.* 17,012, a chair of state is shown with its box seat ornamented with linen panels of the one-rib pattern.   [2] John Botwright (1443–74), Master of Corpus Christi College, Cambridge, caused the parlour and lower bedrooms to be panelled with linen panelling ornamented with gilt knots. R. Willis and J. W. Clark, *Architectural History of Cambridge*, Cambridge, 1886, vol. i. p. 266.   [3] The work cannot be earlier than 1515 when Wolsey was made a cardinal; and as the arms of Henry VIII and Katherine of Aragon appear, it cannot be later than the date of her divorce.   [4] Since been removed to the Lodge.

sixteenth-century panels from Boughton Malherbe and in the hall of Magdalen College, Oxford, which was wainscoted at considerable expense in 1541. At Great Fulford certain panels are dated 1534, and one is carved with the knot, the badge of the Bourchier[1] family. In some instances, portraits were probably intended, as in the carved heads of a man and woman in the wainscot on the east wall of the dining parlour at Haddon Hall.[2] In these panels the costume of the period of Henry VIII is carefully rendered, and the figure and dress of the man is not unlike that of Sir George Vernon on the tomb of his father at Tong Church.

Another type of ornamented panel is the double-ogee scroll or strap with ornamental fillings of various ornaments (expecially the vine), which was widespread throughout nearly all north-eastern Europe during the late fifteenth century. In the wainscoted room formerly at Boughton Malherbe, the panels are nearly all of this type, but the panels vary in detail, some being enriched with grapes and foliage, others with ornamental cusping. The date of this wainscot (about 1520) is established by a panel bearing the rebus of Wotton surmounted by the initials E. & D., for Edward and Dorothy Wotton, which are linked together by a knot.[3] In the wainscot of flank or a wall formerly in the hall at Halnaker the panels were carved with foliated scrolls; while the doors were linen-panelled. In the panels, knots, scrolls, and devices were mingled with the cognisances of the founder, of Henry VIII. and of Katherine of Aragon.[4]

In the examples hitherto mentioned all the panels have been carved with Gothic or quasi-Italian ornament. In the dining-room at Haddon Hall, however, the panels (with the exception of those just beneath the cornice, which are carved with coats of arms, medallioned heads, linked initials, and other devices) are plain, while during the second half of the sixteenth and seventeenth centuries the panelling was usually of plain framed repeated oblongs. Wainscot of the later Tudor period is plentiful, houses being sometimes lined with oak throughout. In the hall the wainscot was often carried up to about the level of the window sills, other rooms were usually wainscoted from floor to ceiling. A contract between the builder of Hengrave and the carpenter for 'seelying' the house shows that some of the rooms were wainscoted their full height, and others, such as the hall, for a certain number of feet,[5] the intervening space being hung with tapestry or stained cloth, or decorated with plasterwork or painting. At this date, there is no trace of dado or skirting. It might be supposed that the oak for this wainscoting was English grown, but, according to Harrison, 'our wainscot is not made in England'; and it is certain that in the eastern counties, coast towns imported a considerable amount of oak from Norway and Denmark in planks. The oblong panels of this period are framed in narrow stiles, and variety was given to the homogeneous surface by dividing it into sections by pilasters, fluted or carved, or by introducing enriched panels. The pilasters were often enriched with shallow patterns, as in the room from the house in Exeter in the Victoria and Albert Museum, and in the Job room at Bradninch Manor, Devonshire, where each pilaster differs in design. In one, armour in use in the Elizabethan period is set out in trophies; in another, musical instruments. The framework of the panel was sometimes shaped to form a round-headed arch (Fig. 5), a series of such panels forming an arcade; or a composite panel was constructed to include in the centre an inner subsidiary panel, oblong or lozenge-shaped, connected by its stiles with the outer main panel (Fig. 2). In a room at Badminton (Fig. 3), the centre diamond within the oblong panel is emphasized by a projecting faceted lozenge. In the wainscoted great chamber formerly at Gilling (Fig. 2), the panels are divided by stiles into a lozenge-shaped centre and four triangular corner panels. At Carbrook Hall there are two tiers of large panels enclosing smaller square panels, above a tier of plain panels. This composite panel construction was even further elaborated in Holland and Flanders. The general design of the wainscoting of the long gallery at Haddon Hall (1589) is a series of semicircular-headed arches, alternately large and small, divided by pilasters, and crowned by a frieze and rich turreted and embattled cornice. The base of the wainscot is plainly panelled; in the second height the pilasters are fluted, and the spaces between them enriched with geometric devices. The third height is occupied by semicircular arches, and the pilasters are here carved with scale pattern and finished with capitals of foliage filling up the spandrels of the arches. The mouldings of the wainscoting are planted on to the woodwork, and not, as in earlier work, worked in the solid. Later there is a preference for a composite panel rather than arcading, and also for

Room in Upper Floor of House, Norwich. Now destroyed.
Drawn by W. Curtis Green, R.A. Based on a sketch by J. W. Winter, 1849.

skilled joinery with enrichments of split turnings. Such lathe-turned balusters, drops, beads, and spindles, sawn longitudinally, were also applied to woodwork. In a section of wainscot designed by John Smithson for the great chamber at Theobald's, strapwork is applied to the face of the panels, to be painted a 'walnut-tree colour'. Variety is obtained in a few instances by the grouping of two sizes of panel, a long and a short, as in the room from the old Palace, Bromley-by-Bow (1606). At Towneley Old Hall is a small dining-room which is wainscoted with panels set diagonally between the dado and cornice,[1] and a similar arrangement is shown in a room at Park Hall, Shropshire.

    There is a growing architectural bias in wainscoting of the reign of Charles I, which is a proof of the increasing influence of the architect. The wall is treated systematically as an order, divided into bays by pilasters resting upon pedestals and surmounted by a carefully detailed frieze and cornice. The pilasters are not overlaid with ornamental detail, and there is a tendency to use miniature architectural forms, such as a pedimented archway or opening, as ornamental detail, as in the chimney-piece in the

---

[1] This wainscot is dated 1628.

Jerusalem Chamber, Westminster, dating from the reign of Charles I. There are examples of wainscoting with reserved ornament upon salient features such as the chimney-piece and doorways, the Laudian wainscot of St John's College, Oxford, and the wainscoted room formerly in the Reindeer Inn, Banbury. In the latter room the doorway and chimney-piece are treated with broken pediments, and detached columns are placed at the angles of the recess of the bay window; while the wall surface is divided by pilasters.

CONSTRUCTION

The framework of panelling is morticed and tenoned together, and pinned with oak pins. Seasoned wood was required or else, as Shakespeare notices, the pane would warp:—

> This fellow will but join you together as they join wainscot;
> Then one of you will prove a shrunk panel and like green timber, warp, warp.[1]

Mouldings were cut in the solid in early examples; and the mason's mitre is used, that is, the rails abut squarely on to the stiles, and the mouldings are returned and mitred in stone-masons' method. Woodworkers' technique appears, however, in the form of the stopped moulding, in which the mouldings of both vertical and horizontal framing are stopped before the point of junction, as in the hall screen in Haddon Hall. Early in the sixteenth century, however, as in the Waltham Abbey[2] panelling dating from about 1520 the mouldings of the stiles die out before reaching the rails, thus allowing either a vertical or horizontal framing to be moulded in one piece. Later, instead of stopping the moulding, this was carried on to intersect with the moulding, meeting it at right angles, thus forming a mitre; and mitred mouldings, which appear in the panels from Beckingham Hall, dated 1546, were almost universally in use by the close of the sixteenth century. There is a chamfer (or splayed) edge at the bottom of each panel. The framework mouldings of the wainscot of the old Palace, Bromley-by-Bow (1606) which are worked in the solid, project slightly above the surface, and are continued all round the panel, and not splayed at the bottom of each panel as in earlier wainscot. Applied mouldings in which a separate moulding is planted on and glued to the panel was a labour-saving contrivance.

Wainscot was usually coloured until the middle of the seventeenth century. The framework of the panels was frequently painted red, and the panels themselves decorated with designs in various colours. At Bramshill payment was made in 1618 for painting two chambers with 'wallnut culler',[3] but survivals of the original graining, marbling, or other colour schemes are rare. At Boughton Malherbe there were (when Shaw visited it) considerable remains of colour decoration in the drawing-room.[4] The walls throughout were 'panelled with painted wainscot, the styles black with deep blue mouldings, and gilded ornaments at the intersections'. Traces of green and gold paint are still visible on the wainscot of the drawing-room at Haddon Hall, and of surviving examples, the most complete is the Kederminster Library at Langley Church, which was built in 1617, where the panels are painted with strapwork, cartouches, and landscapes (Fig. 12). The Gilt room at Holland House, decorated by Cleyn with the emblems of the Rich family within contoured panels was a room untouched, in essentials, from the days when it was decorated for a fête in the reign of Charles I until its destruction by enemy action.

For wainscoting and interior work, the use of oak is universal, all other woods (in Harrison's words) being neglected, 'nothing but oak any whit regarded'. Oak is a wood of a brown colour varying in shade, and shrinking considerably in seasoning. The young wood of English oak is very tough and does not combine well with glue, whereas foreign oak and that of old trees is more workable.[5] As it is invariably framed up and pinned together by oak pegs, there is no decomposition (as in modern work) owing to the use of iron nails which are corroded by the acid secreted by the wood.[6] It will be found on examining the back of old panels, that the wood has been rent, and as oak can only be cloven on the

---

[1] *As You Like It*, III, iii. 87. [2] In the Victoria and Albert Museum.
[3] Sir W. Cope, *The History of Bramshill*, p. 123. [4] These have now disappeared. [5] Tredgold, *Elementary Principles of Carpentry* (1885), p. 57.
[6] Elwes, J. H., and Henry, *The Trees of Great Britain and Ireland*, p. 340.

line of the medullary rays, this method shows better figure or silver grain than when sawn on the quarter. In many examples, as in the wainscoted room at the old Palace, Bromley-by-Bow, the silver grain is dark brown and raised above the surface of the wood. These richly figured panels were, as Evelyn writes, in request until the importation of the finer-grained Norway oak[1] after the Restoration, and it will be noticed that these veined woods are much in evidence in the panels, where they show to the best advantage.

The English walnut was only planted in the late years of the sixteenth century, while the black walnut[2] was not introduced until about 1656, when it is mentioned among the list of plants grown in the younger Tradescant's garden.[3] Walnut wood, therefore, must have been imported[4]—probably from Southern and Central France[5]—for cabinet work, and its use for wainscot is exceptional.

Pine and fir (soft white woods) appear by records to have been employed, not as in the eighteenth century as painted wall-linings, but in their natural surface. A parlour at Chatsworth is recorded to have been 'fayre waynscoted with white wood' in an inventory of the 'building' Countess of Shrewsbury; and in an inventory taken some time between 1596 and 1609 (or very shortly afterwards), the study in the great chamber of Brooke House, Hackney, is noted as wainscoted with deal.[6] Sir Bulstrode Whitelocke, ambassador to Sweden during the Commonwealth, on his return to England in 1654 brought with him a cargo of deal boards, which he mentions in his journal to have been used at Fawley Court for new flooring his hall and for wainscoting it.

Carving

Decline of Technique in the Early and Middle Tudor Period—The Italian Influence—
The Flemish Influence—Carolean Carving

AFTER the freshness, humour, and vigour of English carving of the thirteenth to the fifteenth century, in which the misericords alone, as has been observed,[7] offer a record of medieval society as the terra-cotta figurines do of Greece, there is a sensible decline in the Early Tudor period both in imaginative handling and often in technique. During the period of Italian influence, English Renaissance ornament, allied with what survived of Gothic, was small in scale. The ornament (which was always described by contemporaries as 'Romayne work' or 'antique') consisted of the *motifs* of the Renaissance, such as medallioned and wreathed heads, cartouches supported by amorini, or grotesques finishing in scrolls (known as 'trails of savage work'), dolphin-headed scrolls, and candelabra. Reduced to its linear elements in upright panels it mainly consisted of an axial line, with a vase or candelabrum as central ornament, and scrolls set symmetrically on either side of it. The handling is far from the suave movement of Italian carving. Some panels of Henry VIII's reign, probably by foreign craftsmen, stand out from the rest of the carving of this period. Of these, the finest (of French character[8]) is that bearing in the centre within a sunk medallion the high relief bust of a king—one of the Nine Worthies. In his right hand he grasps a sword, and on either side of this medallion are crowned shields bearing the royal arms of England. A composition removed from Beckingham Hall, Tolleshunt Major, in Essex (which is supposed to have formed the overpiece to a

---

[1] *Sylva*, Book I, Chap. III. Sec. Mark 17. 'Some pannells are curiously vein'd, of much esteem in former times, till the finer grain'd Spanish and Norway timber came amongst us.' [2] *Juglans nigra.* [3] *Museum Tradescantium* (1656), p. 147. [4] May 1613. 'I recd. out of France, 24 planck of walnuttree.'—'Diary of the Earl of Cork', *Lismore Papers*, vol. i. p. 23. [5] In Evelyn's time black walnut was imported from Virginia, and also from Grenoble. [6] E. A. Mann, *Brooke House, Hackney*, p. 29. [7] E. S. Prior, *Medieval Figure Sculpture in England*, p. 539. [8] Victoria and Albert Museum, 1585-1855 (date about 1530-40).

fireplace in the hall or principal apartment), it is divided into twelve compartments, of which the centre panels of the upper tier contain the arms of Henry VIII and the initials R. H.; the two side panels are carved with a foliated dolphin-headed scroll and inscribed with the text *Humilibus dat graciam* within a cartouche. Divided from the upper tier by three narrow panels is a centre panel carved with the bust of a man in high relief, within a medallion incised with the words *Engratitud est la mort*, the motto of Beckingham. Panels on either side of this contain a similar bust in contemporary costume, set within shaped pediments (on which the date 1546 is incised), which are flanked by dolphin-headed scrolls on which small nude winged figures are perched; while in the lowest tier of narrow panels is a shield of arms supported by griffins, and decorative panels in which foliated acanthus and small nude figures appear.[1] The carving is fine and finished, but there is a naïveté and lack of proportion in detail. Early Renaissance ornament in its richest form is pictured in Hall's description of the temporary banqueting house erected to celebrate the alliance between Henry VIII and François Ier at Greenwich in 1527.[2] 'The jawe peces and crestes were karved with vinettes and trailes of savage worke, and richly gilted with gold and byse, thys woorke corbolying bare the candelstykes of antyke woorke, whiche bare litle torchettes of white waxe. . . . At the nether ende were two broade arches upon thre Antike pillers all of gold, burnished swaged and graven full of gargills and serpentes, supportyng the edifices; the Arches were vawted with Armorie, all of Bice and golde, and above the Arches were made many sondri Antikes and devises.'

In certain panels, usually dating from the close of the reign of Henry VIII, the ornament is evenly distributed over the panel without emphasis upon an axial line, or upon any salient feature.

After essays in the new grammar of Italian ornament, which lost their directing force after the disappearance of the Italians at work on the royal palaces, the English craftsman followed the foreign fashions by means of pattern books. A combination of strapwork[3] and fantastic figures seems to have been developed by Pieter Coeck of Alost; and becomes the universal Low Country vocabulary of ornament in Theodore de Bry[4] and contemporary designers. There is much Tudor carving, marked by the undisciplined elaboration of the subsidiary low relief carving, and the rudeness and rigidity of the modelling of the caryatid figures. In some examples, especially in the West of England, carving invades and overlays all the available space. Its ornament is the weak point of late sixteenth-century decoration and architecture. Strapwork in its developed form combined with grotesques appears in the triumphal arches set up for the reception of Philip of Spain on his entry into Antwerp in 1541, but it is not until the approach of the seventeenth century that strapwork in England runs riot.[5] The cresting of the screens at Trinity College, Cambridge,[6] and at Knole[7] are examples of this ornament, but the most complete is the woodwork of Croscombe Church, where the screen is surmounted by strapwork ornaments reaching almost to the roof, and the sounding board of the pulpit[8] is in the same style. As strapwork appears in the pew-rails of St John's Church, Leeds, which was built between 1631 and 1633, its uninterrupted popularity was of long duration. The aim of the Jacobean craftsman was a Flemish version of the architectural design of the period, in which the mouldings and surfaces are only slightly emphasized by incised or low relief detail. There is an effort to secure the effects of stone and panelled marble in woodwork by rustication, and by the introduction of faceted and oval bosses originally representing a piece of richly veined marble. The utmost that can be said for some such overladen work of the Early Renaissance is that, like the founder's tomb in the London Charterhouse, it, 'with its grotesque carvings, monsters, heraldries, darkles and shines with the most wonderful shadows and light'. While the greater portion of Elizabethan decorative work, when it attempts the magnificent, is coarse in execution, there are instances of crisp carving and skilful handling or ornament, as in the chimney-piece from a house in Oxford formerly owned by the physician Richard

---

[1] Victoria and Albert Museum, W. 33, 1912. [2] *Triumphant Reigne of Kyng Henry VIII* (ed. Whibley), 1904, vol. ii. p. 85. [3] Strapwork seems to have originated in Venice. [4] Theodore de Bry visited England in 1586–87 and again in 1588–89. [5] It appears in the cresting of the fountain in the Great Court, Trinity College, Cambridge, begun in 1602. [6] About 1604–05. [7] *circ.* 1606. [8] Dated 1616.

Slythurst, in the Star Room, from Great Yarmouth, where the modelling of the demi-figures is distinct from the usual crude cutting of the period, and in the fine caryatid figures in the upper stage of the chimney-piece formerly at Lambourn Hall, in Essex. It is significant that the two last examples are from the Eastern Counties. To a vigorous school of carving at Exeter in Elizabeth's reign must be assigned the graceful running ornament and arabesques in the pilasters and skirting of an old house at Exeter,[1] and on the pilasters at Bradninch Manor, in which arabesques, trophies of arms, and musical instruments are deftly arranged. In many examples, the sense of texture and lavishness of invention recalls the intricacies of medieval Devonian screens.

In the reign of Charles I there is less use of the simple device of unmodelled strapwork, and what ornament there is is concentrated and marshalled. An instance of the new architectural bias in decoration was the white parlour in Holland House (where the pedimented centres of the panels were decorative points), and the Laudian work in St John's College, Oxford.

Inlay

Inlay of Woods, and of Compressed Shavings—Parqueting

INLAYING, or the laying of small pieces of wood in hollows cut out of the surface of another wood, is an alternative to carved enrichment, but during the late sixteenth and the early seventeenth century was used chiefly in connexion with carving. Saw-cut slices of contrasting woods, such as holly or poplar (for light tones) and bog oak (for dark), with an occasional insertion of a reddish-coloured wood, such as cherry, form the ornament. In the inlaid chamber[2] from Sizergh Castle, poplar and bog oak are used for the enrichment of the wainscot, which is divided horizontally into dado (consisting of one large composite panel), a panelled arcading. This arcading is divided by pilasters into bays, within which the long panels are inlaid with foliated arabesques in poplar, in the centre of some of which strips of inlay form an interlaced lozenge; the links in the scroll work and details are in bog oak. In the panels of the surbase, strips of inlay forming geometrical or arabesque patterns are used. The arabesques of the panels in the arcading of the Sizergh panelling have no close parallel, though the two upper tiers of panels in the drawing-room at Gawthorpe are enriched with a conventional inlay, and the frieze and uppermost tier of arcaded panels in the dining-room at Sydenham House, Devonshire, are also inlaid with arabesques. In the Smithson drawings in the Coke Collection is a sketch for a screen, in which certain panels are designed for inlay.[3]

A favourite subject for inlay was the elevation of a fantastic building, such as in the chimney-piece, dated 1594, illustrated in *Ancient Woodwork and Ironwork in Cambridge*,[4] in which the panels are inlaid with coloured woods to represent a temple or pavilion with domes or cupolas. Inlay also takes the form of interlacing linear forms, or of flowers, as in the wainscot from the great chamber, Gilling, or the chimney-piece at Levens, where each panel is inlaid with varied geometrical patterns in narrow lines of bog oak and light wood within the centre panel. The four corners are also inlaid with flowers in the same woods. Some rare examples of an inlay of compressed shavings are found in the eastern counties. The frieze and fascia of the chimney-piece formerly at Lambourn Hall, Essex, which is dated 1571, is enriched with bandings of shavings compressed with glue. The frieze of the panelled ground floor room at the Old House, Sandwich, is inlaid with oblongs of this same material, of which the

---

[1] Victoria and Albert Museum, 4870–4881, 1856.　[2] *circ.* 1575. In the Victoria and Albert Museum.　[3] No. 47, Coke Collection.　[4] W. B. Redfarn and J. W. Clark, Cambridge, 1881–86, Plate 4.

columns of the upper stage of the chimney-piece are made. In the centre of the two panels are framed small figure subjects, inlaid upon a light ground.

Parqueting for flooring was used, according to Aubrey, in Sir John Danvers's[1] house at Chelsea, of which the drawing-room floor was 'checquered like a chesse board of Box and Ewgh panels of about six inches square'.[2]

Plaster

Design of Plaster—Foreign Sources of Design—Local Centres—Colour Decoration—Ingredients

THE chief use of the 'plastique art', was in England the 'graceful fretting of roofes', and Sir Henry Wotton alludes to its durability and cheapness. The art was introduced in Henry VIII's reign by Italian craftsmen who were engaged on the plaster statues and bas-reliefs on the exterior of Henry VIII's palace of Nonsuch. The Gothic joiners' craft that first influenced the design of plasterwork, and their flat timber ceilings, divided by moulded rectilinear ribs ornamented with a carved boss at the intersections, governed the setting out of the earliest extant Tudor plaster-work. In the ceiling in Cardinal Wolsey's closet at Hampton Court the rectilinear wooden ribs enclose *papier-mâché* fillings of delicate design, centring in a badge, such as the Tudor rose or ostrich feathers. Round the walls on two sides is a frieze bearing the Cardinal's motto, '*Dominus michi adiutor*', and badges in roundels varied by ornament in the Italian style. In the ceiling of the chapel of St James's Palace, in which the date 1540 occurs, the panels are divided by gilt wooden ribs, and a small running ornament, cast in lead, enriches the under side of the ribs. The panels contain coats of arms emblazoned in their proper colours, and foliage.[3] In the coved plaster ceiling at Holcombe Court, built in the latter part of the reign of Henry VIII, is a design formed of shallow ribs, and a number of pateræ are intro-duced, each containing one of the letters of the name of the builder, Sir Roger Bluet, enclosed in a wreath.

With the use of plastic material for the ribs in the ensuing period there was no necessity for a rectilinear setting-out; and the designs may be divided into geometrical schemes ranging from the simplest to elaborate compositions and including every shape of panel, curved, angular, and interlaced, and into free designs, either of interlaced strapwork or of all-over floral ornament. In a pattern book for glazing[4] the author claims in the title-page that his 'draughtes' are 'not impertinent for Plasterers', and his more elaborate designs are suitable for geometrical setting-out. Moulded plasterwork is usually on a flat ceiling, but it is not unusual to find the panels curving downwards at intersections to form a pendant, which adds variety to the surface. The ornament is softly modelled, free from undercutting and sharp projections, and melting into the background. In Elizabethan examples, narrow ribbing, closely following the mouldings of timber construction, appears. This early work which has character is appropriate to the small rooms. The repeated ornamental *motifs* radiate from the mitred angles of the moulded ribs, and isolated ornaments, badges, rosettes, formal sprays, and fleurs-de-lys are also placed in the centre of the panels. In small rooms a central treatment was used, such as a square or diamond-shaped panel with foliated terminals. It is evident, from the number of houses in which plasterwork still remains, that the output of modelled plaster must have been very great during that great building period, the last quarter of the sixteenth and the first quarter of the seventeenth centuries.

[1] Died 1655.   [2] Aubrey MS., *Natural History of Wilts.*, Bodleian Library.   [3] A view of the ceiling is given in Richardson's *Architectural Remains of the Reigns of Elizabeth and James I*, 1838, Plate 12. It was repaired in 1836 by Sir. R. Smirke.   [4] *A Booke of Sundry Draughtes, Principally Serving for Glaziers, etc.*, by Walter Gedde, London, 1615.

The deep coloured frieze in the presence chamber at Hardwick Hall stands alone in its broad pictorial rendering of landscape and figure subjects; for in this large room Diana and her attendants are seen hunting with dogs and spears amid a forest of trees which shelter animals of the chase, including stags, lions, and elephants. The modelling of the human figure is in advance of the period.

In the reign of James I the ribs assumed a wider, shallower form, enriched with minute floral and scrolling ornament, as is shown in the ceilings from Albyns and Boston House, and in the detail of Great St. Helens. The ribs enclose in the panel spaces heraldic badges, flowers, strapwork, rosettes, formal floral designs, or medallions containing animals and heads. A ceiling in the drawing-room at Canons Ashby is characteristic of the second quarter of the seventeenth century. The larger panels are filled with conventional thistle sprays, the small panels with a draped head; and in a large panel over the chimney-piece are the arms of the Dryden family. The central pendant consists of four human headed scrolls, forming a shaft for a lamp. The ceiling formerly at the Reindeer Inn, Banbury, is also an example of fine Carolean work. The moulded ribs are enriched with delicate scroll ornament which has been outlined with a modelling tool, which helps to give it sharpness and strength. The formal ornament of fantastic scrollwork and figures within the panels shows traces of gilding. The contemporary ceilings at Aston Hall,[1] especially that of the long gallery, are remarkable for the skilful handling of the formal ornament.

Strapwork of an all-over design without panel ribbing consists of a flat interlacing ribbon or scroll in low relief, studded with small jewellings, rosettes, and discs, as in the small drawing-room (formerly the King's room) at Apethorpe, in rooms at Audley End, and at Beckington Abbey. This type of ceiling dates from the first quarter of the seventeenth century.

Characteristically English is a free floral design, for example, the waggon-vaulted gallery at Burton Agnes, which has a scrolling design of exceptional vigour. In a room at Speke the ceiling area is crossed by large main beams, encased in plaster, and enriched with a running design of hops, small in scale, while the panels are filled with a design of interlacing scrolls of rose, vine, and other flowers branching from a central stem whose springing is marked by a strapwork ornament.

In the reign of James I, allegorical personifications appear with greater frequency on the ceiling. The setting of the state-room ceiling at Boston House is an arrangement of linked square and oblong panels broken into semicircular and segmented cuspings, and filled with strapwork cartouches in which are emblematic and fanciful figures. Later the allegorical figures grew to life size, and occupied the central panel of ceilings, as at Forde Abbey, where this newly introduced style was evidently imperfectly understood by country craftsmen, who modelled the figure subjects with a heavy hand, and used ornamental detail several sizes too large. The use of wide ribs ornamented with a guilloche enclosing a large central panel is also a feature of an interesting small house, Slyfield (Fig. 15). A bedroom has a ceiling enriched, enclosing within a large oval wreath of bay the figure of Peace. A more elaborate ceiling in the great chamber has in the cove an intricate all-over design of festoons of drapery and fruit, in which winged amorini and gryphons figure. In the centre is an amorino surrounded by a wreath of laurel.

What influence the Italians may have had disappeared by the reign of Elizabeth; and the names of the plasterworkers that have so far been recorded are English. John Hethe or Heath, who was probably employed by Henry VIII at Nonsuch, leaves to his second son Laurence 'my moldes and molded work that I served the Kinge withal',[2] showing that the moulds were a possession of value, the craftsman's working capital.[3] A certain John Williams is known to have carried out plasterwork at Longleat, and an Abraham Smith, a plasterer, was one of the permanent employees at Hardwick Hall. The ceilings at Knole are the work of the King's plasterer, Richard Dangan, who was paid in 1609 for 'fretts and other work done'; and John Cobbe is paid in 1601 for the 'frettishing' of the ceiling of the great

[1] circ. 1635.　[2] Archæologia, vol. xxxix. p. 34. Heath's will is dated 1st August 1552.　[3] The plasterer submitted 'models' directly to his employer. State Papers, Domestic, Elizabeth, vol. cclxxvi., No. 37.

chamber and long gallery at St John's College, Cambridge. Records of the name of craftsmen are, however, extremely rare. The sources of figure subjects can, in many instances, be traced to pattern books engraved by Flemish artists, which English plasterers adapted to their technique and to the spaces to be filled, simplifying, adding, and eliminating as they worked. In the case of the overpieces to the chimney-pieces at Hardwick Hall (which are the work of Abraham Smith, who worked for the 'building' Countess of Shrewsbury)[1], the design is borrowed from Martin de Vos's four elements— Ignis, Aer, Aqua, Terra—which were engraved by the elder van de Passe. Cast medallion heads of the Nine Worthies by Nicolas de Bruyn appear in several positions, as in the state room from the old Palace, Bromley-by-Bow,[2] Balcarres House in Scotland, and elsewhere. In the Bromley-by-Bow ceiling the centres of six quatrefoils are occupied by medallions bearing the helmeted head and bust of the Worthies, Joshua, Hector of Troy, and Alexander. De Bruyn's plates of this series are dated 1597, but the heads of the Worthies continued to be used as *motifs* in the early seventeenth century. Variants on designs for the Five Senses occur in several early seventeenth-century houses. The Senses are symbolized as follows:—

Hearing (auditus) represented by a woman playing a guitar, surrounded by musical instruments and attended by a stag.

Smelling (olefactus), a woman seated, with vases of flowers and a dog.

Seeing (visus), a seated woman holding a mirror, attended by an eagle.

Tasting (gustus), a seated woman holding a basket of fruit.

Touching (tactus), a seated woman holding a bird which pecks her.

These subjects occur on the ceiling of the Queen's boudoir at Kew Palace (which was built by Samuel Fortrey in 1631); on the upper stage of a chimney-piece in the assize courts, Bristol; and in the state room on the first floor at Boston House, Brentford, dated 1623. Here sixteen panels contain a symbolical figure modelled in relief against a tinted background; and besides the Senses, Time and the elements, Fire and Water, Peace and War, Faith, Hope, and Charity are represented. The devices on the end of the gallery at Little Moreton Hall, representing the Wheel of Fortune, appear in the *Castle of Knowledge*, printed by Reynold Wolfe, 1556.[3] At Blickling (1619-20) the gallery ceiling has in the large panels emblematic figures, of which some appear in Peacham's *Minerva Britanna*[4]; and in a ceiling in an old house in Gravel Lane, Houndsditch, now demolished, the panels are enriched with moral and religious emblems.[5]

Work of similar general design is not infrequently found in various parts of England, but ornament cast from the same moulds is rarely met with.

The frieze from the old Bromley-by-Bow Palace (1606) has been used again at Bury Hall (1615), Edmonton, on the soffit of a beam; the ceiling of another room at Bury Hall has been cast from the same mould as the dining-room ceiling of the Vicarage, Tottenham (1620); the frieze from Albyns is used again in a bedroom at Broughton Castle, Oxfordshire. There are also noticeable similarities in workmanship in certain localities. The ceiling of the drawing-room at Gawthorpe Hall, Lancashire, is similar in character to the work of Speke Hall in the same county; in both houses the design in certain panels consists of a whorl of conical bunches of grapes. In North Devon there are indications of a local centre; and the same frieze is to be seen at Bideford, at Weare Gifford, and at Barnstaple. 'A similar type of design is to be observed between ceilings at Barnstaple and North Molton; cast sprays are to be found reused in wholly different designs, the same moulds being used again and again. The best examples date from between 1590 and 1630, with some minor work as late as 1660';[6] some designs from the sketch book of John Abbott of Barnstaple (1640–1727), which is preserved by his descendants, show the conservative character of West-country plasterwork.[7]

[1] *Archæologia*, vol. lxiv.   [2] In the Victoria and Albert Museum.   [3] Garner and Stratton, *Domestic Architecture during the Tudor Period*, vol. ii. p. 150. [4] Henry Peacham, *Minerva Britanna, or of Garden of Heroical Deuises furnish'd and adorned with Emblems and Impresas of sundry natures. . . .*   [5] Illustrated in C. J. Richardson, *Studies from Old English Mansions* (4th series), London, 1848.   [6] Bruce Oliver, *Devonshire Association*, vol. xlix. (1917) p. 196. [7] 'A Seventeenth-century Plasterer', *Country Life*, March 2nd, 1940.

Pendants of various sizes were developed from the conical bosses which served to cover the mitreing of the intersecting ribs, a joint always difficult to the inexpert; and were employed also for their value in enriching and breaking up the surface of the ceiling, especially in the case of monotonous and low-relief strapwork, as in the fish room, Audley End. Certain pendants are in skeleton form, plastered upon an iron core, as in the great chamber at Herringstone, in Dorset. Plaster was treated with colour and gilding during the Tudor, and continued to be coloured in the ensuing period. At Boughton Malherbe the drawing-room, when Shaw[1] described it, showed a complete colour decoration in the ceiling 'presumed to be one of the most beautiful specimens of embellishment in the kingdom, the ground is white, and the interlaced pattern blue and reddish brown, judiciously intermingled'. The prevalence of colouring is evidenced by the statute of the first years of James I's reign, in which it is enacted that 'no plaisterer shall exercise the art of a painter in the city or suburbs or lay any colour or painting whatsoever, unless he be a servant or apprentice to a painter, or have served seven years' apprenticeship to that trade'. The undercoating of ceilings enriched with modelled plaster contains an amount of cob and clay bound by brown hair; and on this is applied ornamental details and a coating of plaster probably compounded in the following manner: Lumps of lime were slaked with water, and 'as the lime slacked more water was added and the face of the heap smoothed over: as the heat increased this face cracked, but was again and again smoothed over keeping the heat in until the slacking process was completed.' This slaked lime was kept at least twelve or eighteen months before use, and was then mixed with silver or light-coloured sand and plenty of white hair.[2]

Interior Features

The Staircase—The Chimney-piece—The Interior Porch and Door

STAIRCASES of the 'vyse' (or winding) newel type, narrow and steep in gradient and devoid of ornament, continued in use during the fifteenth and first half of the sixteenth centuries, but there was no development of the newel stair, as in France, of wide, stately, and intricate construction. With the introduction of the wooden construction, the stair became the joiner's, not the mason's, province, and developed on lines of its own. There was no intermediate type between the stone spiral and the straight flight of wood, and it is difficult to imagine a possible intermediary. It was not until the latter part of the sixteenth century that spacious and convenient staircases were constructed. The new type of staircase was fitted into a square chamber, contained in a tower which is often a noticeable exterior feature. Its short straight flights are usually worked round a central well, though they are sometimes carried round a solid rectangular block of masonry. Dispensing with the support of the parallel walls, the stair had to be provided with a handrail on its unenclosed side. The stairs were let into strings, which were framed into newels which supported the whole framework. In such a staircase the easy flights were broken by landings or half-paces, and Wootton recommends half-paces to be distributed 'at competent distances for reposing on the way'. Such a system of short flights implies a small staircase hall, since the flights extend only from wall to half-pace. The breadth of the stair was, according to Wootton, not only to avoid encounters, but to 'gratify the beholder'. Over the foot of the first flight and across the staircase hall is sometimes through an arcade (as at Knole), which adds dignity to the approach (Fig. 19). The plan known as the 'dog-legged', in which each flight returns back alongside the flight immediately below it, occupies less space than the preceding, as no

[1] *Details of Elizabethan Architecture*, 1834, p. 19. [2] Bruce Oliver, *Devonshire Association*, vol. xlix. (1917) p. 197.

open well-hole is enclosed. The breadth of the stair, its easy ascent, and the series of newels crowned with finials, have often a striking effect. The component parts were massive in the extreme, the balusters heavy as bedposts, and the handrail stout as a parapet top. Occasionally the newel posts were carried up to support the landing overhead. Arches were sometimes placed between these continuous newels, thus enclosing the staircase well, and this treatment is found at Burton Agnes and Audley End. When free, the newel post was carried above the handrail, and finished with a shaped top, or with carved or turned finials. These finials were sometimes little more than knobs or balls, but in the great staircases tall vase-like forms, obelisks, and pedestals made their appearance. In addition, newels were sometimes completed below by a pendant or drop, following much the same lines as the finials inverted. Human figures as finials were frequent in great houses. At Cromwell House, Highgate, the newels support carved figures of soldiers which appear to date from about 1635. At Bacon's house, formerly standing at Gorhambury, there was, according to Aubrey, a 'delicate staircase of wood which was curiously carved, and on the post of every interstice was some pretty figure, as a grave divine with his book and spectacles, a mendicant friar, and not one twice'. Sir Henry Slingsby, in describing his staircase at Red House, Yorkshire, writes that 'upon every post a crest is set of one of my especial friends, and of my brothers-in-law'. At Hatfield the newels are surmounted by amorini holding various objects, and by lions supporting shields. The outer surface of the string was usually carved or moulded. There were various devices for filling in the space between the newels, of which the turned baluster was the most popular. Another device was balusters shaped from flat pieces of wood, or a series of arches springing from columns and raking upwards with the stair's ascent, or openwork panels, carved in strapwork designs. This filling developed during the reign of Charles I into a modified strapwork, to which interest is given by the inclusion of cartouches and trophies of arms, such as we find in the staircases at Aldermaston dating from 1636 (Fig. 16), Castle Ashby (Figs. 17, 18), and at Cromwell House, Highgate. Rustication of the newels and balustrade in imitation of stonework is met with at Rawdon House, Hoddesden (Figs. 19, 20). Many staircases at present plain were probably painted, and traces of colour are still visible on a staircase at Aston Bury.

In a few instances, as for example at the Hospital of the Blessed Trinity, Guildford, Haddon Hall, Hatfield, Slyfield, and at Oakwell Hall, the original gate placed across the stairs to prevent the dogs from roaming beyond the ground floors has been preserved.

THE CHIMNEY-PIECE

The chimney-piece became a central feature of the room after the introduction of the recessed fireplace and chimney. In the early sixteenth century the flat four-centred arch continued in use, and the chimney-piece was often ornamented in the spandrels, and had the jamb mouldings stopped high above the floor level upon a moulded plinth. The design for a chimney-piece by Holbein in the British Museum is exceptional for its date, and is an early forerunner of the large two-storeyed chimney-pieces of the second half of the sixteenth and early seventeenth century, but special treatment was at times given to the wainscot panels immediately above the fire opening. In a Tudor chimney-piece formerly in the Tankard Inn, Ipswich,[1] curious sculptured panels above the fire opening, representing the Judgment of Paris, are flanked by balusters and surmounted by an entablature. The chimney-piece became an object of display during the Elizabethan period, and the date of its erection, the owner's personal history, and the sum of his experience in some wise saw were sometimes recorded upon its surface. The more important examples of stone and marble were contracted for independently from foreign craftsmen or monumental masons. The note-books of Nicholas Stone[2] record him as supplying

[1] Formerly the residence of Sir Anthony Wingfield, and later removed to Holywells, Ipswich. [2] He records having made chimney-pieces for several seats, including Tart Hall, and a white marble chimney-piece for the Queen's bedchamber at Somerset House in 1631, chimney-pieces for Bagshott Lodge, and for Sir John Wolstenholme at Stanmore, Middlesex. In 1632 a marble chimney-piece was sent to Oxnead (Sir Edmund Paston) costing £80. Stone sent chimney-pieces to Quidenham, in Norfolk, also to Newborough, in Yorkshire, for Sir Henry Belasyse. . . . A. E. Bullock, *Some Sculptural Works of Nicholas Stone, Statuary*, London, 1908.

his clients with chimney-pieces. In an agreement between Lord Cork, in 1639, and a Bristol freemason and carver, Christopher Watts, the latter contracts to make him 'a very fair chimney' for his parlour, which is to 'reach up close to the ceiling with coat of arms complete, with crest, helmet, coronet, supporters and mantling, and foot-pace, which he is to set up and finish at his own charges, fair and gracefull in all respects'.[1]

Hooded chimney-pieces (which had been characteristic of the thirteenth and fourteenth centuries) were rarely built during the early Renaissance. There is, however, a series at Bolsover, showing a variety of plan, and a chimney-piece in an upper room at Upper Swell is also of the hooded type.

The chimney-piece of the early Renaissance projects but little into the room. The chief changes from the Tudor type were the abandonment of the four-centred stone arch for a rectangular opening during the latter half of the sixteenth and seventeenth centuries and the free use of the orders and caryatid figures. In many districts where stone was not available, wood was used with an inner lining of stone, especially towards the close of the sixteenth and early seventeenth centuries. In the simplest form the overpiece is divided into two or three compartments, which are filled by arched, composite, or carved panels. The orders, which were used recklessly and without knowledge, appear in a stone chimney at Boughton, set up by Sir Edward Montagu before his death in 1556. The more important designs consist of two tiers or stages; in the lower, columns standing on pedestals support an entablature, which again supports a lighter and more decorated order. Three-storeyed chimney-pieces, such as the massive structure in the hall at Burton Agnes, are of rare occurrence. In this chimney-piece, which is of stone and marble, coupled Ionic columns, covered with floral scrollwork, support an entablature and upper stage, in which the panel is carved with the parable of the Wise and Foolish Virgins, flanked by female caryatids. Above this stage are three armorial panels[2] with terminal figures between them, the whole of the design being of exceeding richness. (A later pediment includes the arms and quarterings of Sir Griffith Boynton[3] in a shield in the middle).

Pilasters and caryatid figures often take the place of columns. Single or paired, male and female, overlaid with profuse strapwork, jewelled bosses, clamps and bunches of fruit, these strange figures are the Lares of the hearth during the period of the full Flemish influence. The upper stage, if it did not reach the ceiling, was occasionally crowned with an openwork cresting, as in the Great Hall at Audley End. The enclosed panels of the upper tier were filled in, according to the discretion of the owner, with his shield of arms surrounded by mantling which effectively filled the rectangular space allotted to it, with strapwork compositions of Flemish inspiration, with inlay in wood,[4] or with a figure subject framed like a picture. The chimney-piece was thus the most personal feature in decoration. Illustrations from the Bible, such as the Parable of the Wise and Foolish Virgins,[5] the Sacrifice of Isaac, the Three Children,[6] and the story of Job,[7] are met with. The strapwork compositions in Devon and Somerset are often wrought in plaster. The most remarkable instances of grotesques are found in the drawing-room at Boston House,[8] and in the white drawing-room and the south-east bedroom, Charlton House, in which the little palm-bearing human grotesques, sea-horses, and mermaids are from the designs of Abraham de Bruyn (page 9).

In the late Jacobean period a bellied mantel mould usual in contemporary Flemish designs is found, as in the chimney-piece in the drawing-room at Canons Ashby, and in the long gallery at Albyns (Fig. 10). Emblematic figures also figure in shell-headed niches, as in the President's drawing-room, St John's College, Oxford, and in the oak room and long gallery from Albyns. Faith and Hope, and the pair, Peace and Plenty, continue in favour after the reign of James had closed, and in the hall, Boringdon, Devon, the chimney-piece still bears these hopeful emblematic figures, though it is dated two years before the outbreak of the Civil War. The presence of strapwork (which overran the country

[1] *Lismore Papers* (ed. Grosart), vol. v. p. 84. [2] Bearing arms of Sir Thomas Boynton (1544–82) and his third wife, Alice Frobisher, and his fourth, Alice Tempest, displayed in three panels. [3] Who lived at Burton Agnes, 1761–78. [4] The old house, Sandwich. [5] The hall, Burton Agnes. [6] The Shadrach room, Stockton House. [7] The Job room, Bradninch. [8] 1623.

during the early seventeenth century), the use of curved and broken pediments and of decorated pedimented frames, or elaborately moulded panels filling the centres of the overmantel panels, is characteristic of this last phase of Jacobean work; while uninterrupted tapering pilasters and columns replace the earlier caryatid figures.

Chimney-pieces of wood during the sixteenth and early seventeenth centuries were usually decorated in colour and gilding, though very few examples show the original colour scheme. The chimney-piece in the Governor's room at the Charterhouse is parcel gilt and marbled, and the chimney-piece in the gallery at Yarnton also has its original colour and gilding. Material affected the design of chimney-pieces; and alabaster and marble being the province of the monumental mason, the effect of contrasting colourings, such as of black and veined or of black and white panelled marbles, was sought, rather than fanciful sculpture or ornament. As has been pointed out, these panelled marble chimney-pieces, which are only found in great houses such as Knole, Hatfield, and Bramshill, were the work of foreign craftsmen settled in England, such as the Cuers, Colt, and de Witt, who imported their materials through the Low Countries. Colt is paid money on account of three chimney-pieces at Hatfield[1] in 1609 (including, doubtless, the marble example in James I's room), while there are several chimney-pieces at Knole of exceptional quality and design, such as the example in the Reynolds room, composed of panelled and carved marble; and in the Cartoon gallery (Fig. 4) and in the Ballroom, in which the delicately sculptured detail of the upper stage, consisting of trophies, vases, and festoons, is relieved against a ground of black Bethersden marble. In the correspondence relating to the building of Cobham[2] Hall in Kent, it is suggested that Giles de Witt, a 'Dutchman',[3] should be 'set to work either on some new chimney-piece or his lordship's father's tomb, that he may maintain himself', and the marble example in the picture gallery at Cobham Hall (dated 1599) is characteristic of its Flemish source in the bold projection of its relief and technique. In the saloon of Charlton House, Kent, a chimney-piece, of which the upper stage is of panelled marble, while in the lower the supports are figures of Vulcan and Venus, also shows a strong admixture of Low Country realism and finish somewhat later in date.

THE INTERIOR PORCH AND DOOR

The device of throwing forward a porch enclosing the main door of the room was employed where the entrance was from a narrow stair-landing, or as in independent means of access between two communicating rooms. The provision of two doors also excluded draughts. An interior porch, a linen-panelled structure with a Gothic cresting, is shown in Holbein's Basel Drawing of the household of Sir Thomas More. There are examples of inner porches at Cothele, Broughton Castle Stockton House, Sherborne Castle (where there is a pair in one room), Maxstoke, Bradfield, Bradninch Manor and Montacute. In the inner porch of the Job room at Bradninch, the shafts of the columns which rest upon arcaded bases are carved, and the entablature which breaks forward over them is surmounted by small sculptured figures and a strapwork cresting. The interior porch at Bradfield is also an example of rich close-set Devonshire surface carving and figure-sculpture in relief in the arcaded upper stage. The porch from the inlaid chamber formerly at Sizergh Castle (by which a small room in the Dein-court Tower could be reached without passing through the banqueting hall[4]) is semi-octagonal in plan, with a fluted frieze surmounted by cornice, which supports compartments set in an architectural frame, supported by fluted columns. Above this rises a dome, surmounted by a figure of a boy bearing a shield. The interior porch at Broughton Castle is surmounted by pinnacles and by a coat of arms in a pinnacled frame.

[1] Algernon Cecil, *Life of Robert Cecil, 1st Earl of Salisbury*, p. 329. [2] *State Papers, Domestic, Elizabeth*, vols. cclxxxii., No. 64; cclxxix., No. 94. [3] Actually a Fleming, he was born at Bruges. Kirk, 'Returns of Aliens in London' (*Proc. Soc. Huguenot*), 1709, p. 445. [4] Victoria and Albert Museum. *The Panelled Rooms*, No. IV, 'The inlaid room from Sizergh Castle', p. 23.

THE DOOR

Scale 5" to 1'

From the Norwich House of William Lowth, Prior of Walsingham, 1505–1515. Inscribed on the rails: MARIA PLENA GRACIE MATER, MISERICORDIE REMEMBYR WILLYĀ LOWTH PRIOR XVIII.

Minor doors in the early Tudor period were usually straight into the wainscot, and when closed, only distinguishable from it by the presence of hinges. In important rooms in the late sixteenth and early seventeenth century the door became an ornamental feature second only to the chimney-piece, and was often flanked with columns or pilasters supporting an entablature, or in an ornamental composition.

As the door was made up of panels, the number of its panels depended upon the size of the panel which was the unit of the wall covering. Where a large panel was the unit, the door would be made up of a few similar panels; with a small panel as the unit, the door would contain six, eight, or nine panels, as in the door in the interior porch of the Abbot's parlour at Thame, or a door formerly at Boughton Malherbe, which has nine panels. There are instances, however, the door panels of a larger size and more intricate design than the wainscot panels of the room, as in the doorway of the President's drawing-room, St John's College, Oxford, where two large panels of the door are of rich design, the upper a composite mitred panel, the lower containing a faceted boss.

Glazing of Windows

The Bay Window—The Importation of Glass in the Reign of Elizabeth—Glazing—Ventilating Quarries—Stained and Painted Glass Panels and Medallions

A STRIKING feature of early Renaissance domestic architecture was the window, especially the large bay, which, introduced towards the close of the fourteenth century and increasing in size until the time of Henry VIII, was externally a commanding feature, and internally lent variety and interest to the hall or chamber it lighted. Until the reign of Henry VIII glass, except in churches and gentlemen's houses, was a rarity, horn or framed blinds of cloth or canvas (called fenestrals) being used instead. By the close of the sixteenth or the beginning of the seventeenth century, glazing cheapened, and became so plentiful in the reign of Elizabeth that horn was 'quite laid downe'. It was still, however, carefully preserved, and as late as 1567 was removed from Alnwick Castle when its owner was absent lest it should suffer from 'extreme winds'.[1] Different qualities of glass

---

[1] 'Because throwe extreme winds the glasse of the windows of this and other of my lord's castles and houses here in the countrie dooth decay and waste, yt were good the whole leights of everie windowe at the departure of his Lordshippe . . . were taken doune and lade up in safety.' Quoted in Preface, *The Earl of Northumberland's Household Book* (1827), p. xvii.

2   The Great Chamber, Gilling Castle, Yorkshire, showing plaster ceiling of fan and pendant type and frieze painted with scenes and shields of arms, and the heraldic glass dated 1585—*vide* Fig. 31 (now largely dismantled)

3 The Oak Room, Badminton, Gloucestershire, *circa* 1625.
(The wainscot removed from Raglan Castle)

4 The Cartoon Gallery, Knole, Sevenoaks, Kent, early seventeenth century.
The marble chimney-piece in two stages and the ceiling divided by enriched serpentine ribs

5 The Oak Parlour, Quenby Hall, Leicestershire, early years of seventeenth century. The walls divided by pilasters into compartments of four tiers of arched panels

6 The State Drawing-room, Quenby Hall, Leicestershire, *circa* 1620

7   The Hall, Hatfield House, Hertfordshire, showing the screen, *circa* 1610

8   The Hall, Montacute House, Somerset, *circa* 1599

9   Plaster panel in the Hall representing "riding the Skimmington"

10   The Long Gallery, Albyns, Essex, *circa* 1620 (now removed). The doorways date from the early eighteenth century

12   The Kederminster Library, 1617, the panels painted with cartouches, and with heraldic
decoration and symbolical figure on chimney-piece

11   The screen to the Kederminster Pew (1617) in the North Transept,
showing painted and marbled decoration

LANGLEY MARISH CHURCH, BUCKINGHAMSHIRE

13   Crewe Hall, Cheshire, 1616–1632. The Great Hall (destroyed)
From a water–colour by Joseph Nash, circa 1850

14 The Dining-room, Forde Abbey, Dorset, *circa* 1655–58

15 The South Room, Slyfield, Surrey, *circa* 1650, showing panelling divided by pilasters and plaster ceiling centring a figure of Plenty

16   The Staircase, Aldermaston, Berkshire, 1636 (now destroyed)

From Joseph Nash, "Mansions of England," 1869

17 The West Staircase, Castle Ashby, Northamptonshire, *circa* 1635

18 Detail of balustrade

20 Detail of carved panels. Subjects: "Samson and Delilah" and "Musicians"

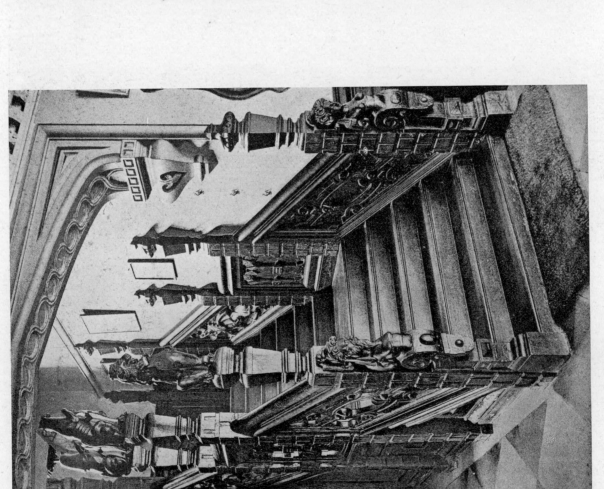

19 The newels rusticated, the tall finials surmounted by turned ornaments and heraldic animals

THE STAIRCASE—RAWDON HOUSE, HODDESDON, HERTFORDSHIRE, DATED 1622

21, 22 (*Left*) Elizabethan Wall Paintings of incidents in the Apocryphal Story of Tobit, *circa* 1555

23 (*Above*) Elizabethan Wall Painting, in the Tobit series

THE WHITE SWAN, STRATFORD-ON-AVON

24 The Staircase, Lees Court, Kent, 1657 (destroyed by fire)

26 Chimney-piece in the house of Sir Thomas Herbert, Pavement, York.
Early seventeenth century

25 The Chimney-piece in the Stone Parlour, Lyme Park, Cheshire, *circa* 1625.
The lower stage of stone

28   Sudbury Hall, Derbyshire, *circa* 1615. Looking into the dining-room from the Hall

27   Interior porch, in Montacute House, Somerset, *circa* 1599

COLLEGE OF ART & CRAFTS.
SUNDERLAND.

29   The Upper stage of the State Room Chimney-piece, Boston House, Brentford, 1623. (The grotesque ornament from a design by Abraham de Bruyn)

30   Upper stage of Chimney-piece, Chicheley, Buckinghamshire. Centre panel carved with a shield of arms (Cave quartering Chester), flanked by carved crests and arched panels

31　Painted Glass, 1585, from the Great Chamber, Gilling Castle, Yorkshire,
by Bernard Dininckhoff. (The window has been removed)

were imported: 'some brought out of Burgundie, some out of Normandie, much out of Flanders, besides that which is made in England, which would be as good as the best, if we were diligent and carefull to bestow more cost upon it'.[1] In 1613 a *Booke of Sundry Draughtes*[2] containing over a hundred designs was published, where (besides the diamond pattern) there are designs based on a combination of geometrical figures. The original designs, giving a rich texture to the window, have in nearly every case been replaced by square or diamond quarries; in Moreton Old Hall, however, the design of the original leaded lights was preserved when they were renewed in the late nineteenth century, and the original patterns closely followed. The lead cames framing the glass panes varied from about three-eighths of an inch to half an inch wide; the casements with their stays and fasteners were of wrought iron. Diamond panes, and intricate variations such as Gedde illustrates, were in general use up to the latter part of the sixteenth century, but in the seventeenth century squares or oblongs were used. Open work quarries of cast lead for ventilation were occasionally introduced among the glazed panes. They occur at Hampton Court and Haddon Hall, and fragments of such leadwork have been found at Fountains Abbey. The bulk of the quarries were filled with white glass, since the admission of light was a prime necessity. So large, however, was the glazed surface, that small panels in coloured glass could be glazed into the quarries without rendering the interior unduly dark. The insertion of coloured glass often took the form of a panel depicting an escutcheon or family badge, with the motto of the family repeated in diagonal lines, as in the hall windows at Ockwells. The effective composition of the royal arms with supporters and mantling was often inserted by loyal subjects in their windows. In the period under Italian influence[3] the ornament consisted of scrolls, candelabra, and grotesques; towards the end of the century strapwork from the Low Countries is prominent, and it is significant that the finest display of glass of this period, from the great chamber of Gilling (Fig. 31), is signed by a Dutch artist, Bernard Dininckhoff. Aubrey[4] writes that the gallery of Gorhambury contained 'glass windows all painted, every pane with several figures of beast, bird, and flower'; but this, and much painted glass of the early Renaissance, has disappeared. In the Betley window the quarries are filled with figures of Morris dancers, and in the centre quarry a Maypole with the legend, 'a mery May'.[5] Enamel painting upon glass came into use about the middle of the sixteenth century, superseding to a great extent the process by which colours, each outlined by leading, were cut out of sheets of pot metal. Enamel painting could, in consequence, disregard the limitations of leadwork, and a whole composition occupy a single sheet of glass. A distinct type of Renaissance glass painting are the minutely finished pictorial medallions painted in various shades of brown and yellow stain, within a wreathed or strapwork border.

In church windows there was a revival of the art of glass painting towards the close of James I's reign, and some Low Country glass painters settled in England, among them Baptista Sutton and the two Van Linges, whose work is seen in Oxford Colleges. The east window of Wadham College Chapel was glazed by Bernard van Linge, a Frieslander, and in this instance not only the executant, but the pot metal was imported from abroad.

The Screen

THE lower end of the hall—that is, the end farthest from the dais—was cut off by a screen from the passage, known as 'the screens', from which access was obtained to the pantry, kitchen, and servants' quarters. The screen stood upon a sill into which the principal uprights were let, and from which they were carried to an upper beam; and cross rails were

[1] Harrison, in Holinshed, vol. i. p. 315.   [2] By Walter Gedde or Gidde.   [3] By an Act, 22 Hen. VIII, c. 13, noblemen and gentry were to be allowed to employ alien joiners and glaziers in their own work without molestation. Quoted in W. Cunningham, *Alien Immigrants*, p. 165.   [4] 'Perhaps his lordship might use them as topiques for locall memory'. *Mem.*, vol. ii. p. 232.   [5] Sold at Sotheby's, June 1922.

also inserted. The screen did not, usually, reach to the roof, and had one or two openings, which were not hung with doors. At Haddon Hall the screen is a substantial wood framing of this character of which the uprights and cross rails are moulded, but the mouldings are stopped before they reach the cross rails. The panels are long and narrow, each being headed with cinquefoil cusping. The screen at Ockwells has a battlemented cornice and tall panels[1] the two openings of which have never been hung with doors.

From the latter part of the sixteenth century to the reign of Charles I, the screen was treated as an opportunity of ambitious design and was, like the chimney-piece, often contracted and bargained for separately. It displays in great houses all the details the craftsmen had found in pattern books in their richest form, the orders, terminal caryatids and fantastic details of all kinds, culminating in a cresting, as at Crewe Hall (Fig. 11). In two-tiered screens there is an upper and richer stage, as at Knole and in Trinity College, Cambridge. The screen was crested with open-work strapwork ornaments of pyramidal outline enclosing shields of arms, or with balustrading. The spaces between the doors were wainscoted, in some cases with panels of richer design than the hall wainscot. In the hall screen at Knole, dating from about 1606, the first stage is surmounted by a gallery, of which the arcades are filled with pierced panels imitating latticework; above the gallery parapet is a strapwork cresting and in the centre an open-work achievement of the Sackville arms and supporters. The carving, which is Flemish in character, is notable for its finish. In the screens of Middle Temple Hall and Trinity College, Cambridge,[2] the intricacy and delicacy of the open strapwork of the cresting and of the arched panels of the upper stage could hardly be surpassed. In smaller buildings the one-storeyed screen was naturally of simpler character. With the discontinuance of its old usage as a common living and dining-room, the hall becomes merely an entrance, and the need for a screen disappears.

---

[1] 4 feet 8½ inches long by 9 inches wide. [2] The work was executed by Francis Carter. '27th April 1603, paid to Francis Carter for parts of his bargayne for the workmanship of a skrene for ye hall'. Willis and Clark, *Architectural History of Cambridge*, vol. ii. p. 492.

II

THE LATE STUART PERIOD (1650-1720)

Introduction : The Interior

The Work of Inigo Jones—The Dutch Influence

FROM the reign of Charles I English domestic architecture follows a development, known as the Later Renaissance, during which the 'incorrect' buildings of the early Renaissance gave way to a scholarly Palladian. In some cases taste was developed by continental travel.[1] Howell claims that the Earl of Arundel 'observing the uniforme and regular way of stone structure up and downe Italie, hath introduced that forme of building to London and Westminster and elsewhere, which though distasteful at first, as all innovations are, yet they find now the commodity, firmness, and beauty thereof the three maine principles of Architecture.'[2] Charles I was 'well skilled in things of antiquity'. He could 'judge of medals whether they had the number of years they pretended unto. . . . He encouraged all the parts of learning and delighted to talk with artists, and with so great a facility did apprehend the mysteries of their professions that he did sometimes say "he thought he could get his living, if necessitated, by any trade he knew of, but making of hangings, although of these he understood much and was greatly delighted in them".'[3] It was by his wish that Webb was trained in architecture. Some French names appear among the architects and artists of this reign, among these Le Sueur supplied the royal figures in the screen designed by Inigo Jones formerly in Winchester Cathedral, and the statues of Charles I and Henrietta Maria at St John's College, Oxford. Signs of the influence of the style of Louis XIII are visible in some English detail, such as the doors of the Hall of Lees Court (Fig. 32). An 'ingenious' architect, Solomon de Caux, was at work at Wilton in 1633; and a book by Isaac de Caux, described as *Ingeneyeur et Architecte*, was printed at London in 1644. But Palladian principles were naturalized in England by Inigo Jones, the most powerful influence in English architecture, who had shown London a complete Palladian building in the Whitehall Banqueting House in the closing years of James I's reign. As part of his Palladian system, the height of rooms was increased, but does not reach the exaggerated scale of the early eighteenth-century architects, who forgot that in England the height of rooms has to be lowered 'in regard to coldness of climate and expense'. The effect of the great height of the double and single cube rooms at Wilton is reduced by a wide cove of quadrant section (Figs. 34, 35). The Wilton chimney-pieces show the imprint of Barbet's designs. Jones leaves the ceiling (or a panel of the ceiling) to be 'richly gilded and painted with story', as in the double cube room at Wilton, in which the full colours of the painting contrast with the white and gold of the walls. His interiors may be judged by his sketches and by his work at Wilton (Figs. 33–35). The new manner was not only apparent in the 'decorum' of the ornament, but in the symmetrical disposition of window openings and doors, and the introduction of definite proportion between the height, width, and length of rooms. He had a preference for the cube. He was followed by Roger Pratt, who after six years' Italian travel, was proficient in Palladian architecture.

The influence of Holland became paramount in England from 1660. Charles II, during the greater part of his exile, lived there; and many royalists spent years there. Dutch commerce between the years 1651 and 1672 seems to have reached its greatest height, and the Dutch controlled almost the entire

[1] For instance, Richard Boyle, first Earl of Burlington (1612–1697), was sent abroad in his twentieth year. He spent over two years visiting France, Flanders, and Italy. [2] *Instructions for Forreine Travell* (1642). [3] Life of Charles I at the end of *Eikon Basilike* (Ed. 1727).

carrying trade of Europe; they were also first in the field in trade with the East, and it has been esti-mated that during the seventeenth century the foreign trade and navigation of Holland was greater than that of the rest of Europe. Interest in Holland was disseminated by a number of travel books pub-lished in the latter half of the seventeenth century, in which the magnificence of the town hall of Amsterdam, the Mauritshuis, and the House-in-the-Wood was recounted at length. 'There is not any state in Europe where the people are so rich as in Holland', according to a visitor in 1701.[1] Owen Feltham speaks admiringly of the costliness of their interior decorations, 'not only in hangings and ornaments, but in pictures which are found even in poorer houses'. Their skilled artisans were ready to emigrate at the decline of this prosperity after 1672, and Dutch carvers and merchants figure in con-temporary accounts and diaries. One Dutch architect, Captain William Wynne (or Winde), practised in England; and the English architects formed a style on Dutch models which was already established be-fore the advent of Wren, with whom it is generally associated. Charles II 'loved planting and building, and brought in a politer way of living which passed to luxury and intolerable expense';[2] the next influential ruler, William III, shared Charles's tastes for building and planting; and in this reign a fuller French influence makes itself apparent. France, under Louis XIV, was the centre of immense activity in architecture and the arts; her influence continued to affect Germany, Italy, Holland, and England, until the late eighteenth century. In England the French influence was less considerable in architecture during the reign of William. Old Montagu House[3] and the first Duke of Montagu's additions to Boughton are remarkable from their isolation from other houses of the date. Both houses were built for Ralph, Earl and afterwards Duke of Montagu, who had a marked French bias and had been am-bassador to Louis XIV. The French influence continued under the reign of Anne, giving place, in the case of some great houses built during this reign, to an Italian feeling, owing to the number of Italian painters and stucco-workers who were brought into the country by architects or patrons.

In great houses, such as Vanbrugh's Castle Howard, Grimsthorpe and Blenheim (Fig. 1, frontis-piece), magnificence is attained by massive planning and size.

These houses were not so large in extent as some of the great late Elizabethan and Jacobean houses, such as Holdenby and Audley End, but the size and height of the state rooms, and especially the hall, was increased. The early stages of Vanbrugh's architectural career are somewhat obscure; Castle Howard and Blenheim belong to the early years of the succeeding century, and he was also employed upon a number of lesser houses, while his style was followed by architects like Wakefield, who worked under him. For the latest of his great houses, Grimsthorpe (1722–1724), he provided the 'biggest entrance hall in the Kingdom'. Though Vanbrugh is a baroque architect, he shows a preference for bare walls. He is more at home in the monumental stonework of the great halls of Castle Howard, Seaton Delaval and Grimsthorpe, than in smaller, domestic rooms. In Grimsthorpe and Seaton Delaval, the hall has rows of arches round the walls; at Castle Howard, Corinthian piers, connected by semi-circular panelled arches, support the cupola. Vanbrugh's tendency to simplification and enlargement of forms can be seen in the hall chimney-piece at Grimsthorpe, and in that in the saloon at Kimbolton.

During this period the enlightened interest taken by the owners and builders of small and great houses is a fact of much significance. The fourth Earl of Devonshire turned from the disappointments of political life to architecture and the arts, which had interested him since the early days of his foreign travel, and to the rebuilding of Chatsworth.[4] In the majority of the great late seventeenth-century

[1] *A New Description of Holland* (1701). [2] Evelyn *Diary*, 4th February 1685. [3] The first Montagu House, burned down in 1686, was designed by Richard Hooke (1635–1703). The second was the work of Puget, and the interior was painted by French decorative painters, De La Fosse, Rousseau, and Monnoyer. [4] Bishop Kennet writes that the Earl 'contracted with Workmen to pull down thd South Side of that good old Seat and to rebuild it in a Plan he gave to them for a front to his Gardens so fair and August that it look'd like a Model only of what might be done in after Ages. When he had finish'd this Part he meant to go no further; till seeing Public Affairs in a happier Settlement, for a Testimony of Ease and Joy, he undertook the East side of the quadrangle & rais'd it entirely new in conformity to the South and seemed then content to say that he had gone half way through and would leave the rest to his Heir. In this resolution he Stop'd about Seven years, and then reassum'd Courage and began to lay the Foundations for two other Sides to complete the noble Square, and these last, as far as Uniformity admits do exceed the others by a West front of most excellent Strength and Elegance, and a Capitol on the North side that is of singular ornament and Service' (The south front was begun 12th April 1687).

houses the name of the architect is unknown; in several cases the design is attributed to the owner. At Hinchingbrooke, the Earl of Sandwich[1] was probably his own architect, though the execution of the work was in the hands of Kennard (the master-joiner at Whitehall), and of Philip Packer, who consulted with Lord Sandwich as to the proposed improvements. The panels of the staircase were brought to Lady Sandwich in London for her approval before being sent down to Hinchingbrooke. The details of the building and decoration of Burley-on-the-Hill were personally overseen by the Earl of Nottingham, who ordered each chimney-piece, the dimensions and colour of which appear to have caused him much correspondence.[2] The Duke of Marlborough found time to write from Brussels in 1708 about the furnishing of his new palace at Woodstock, directing Vanbrugh to finish the breaks between the windows in the great cabinet with looking-glass.[3] The interest was repaid by the extraordinary skill and accuracy of workmanship among the craftsmen, so that at Blenheim 'so perfectly was the work carried out that it is possible to look through the keyholes of ten doors and see the daylight at the end over three hundred feet off'.[4] The Diary of Celia Fiennes, which records her journeys in the reigns of William III and Anne, preserves a picture of many great houses. Of the fourth Early of Devonshire's additions to Chatsworth she writes:—

'The Hall is very Lofty, painted top and sides with armory and there is 18 steps on Each side goes up as an arch, wth Iron Barristers tipt wth gold wch Meetes on ye top Large steps of Stone. Thence you Enter a dineing-roome, two drawing roomes, a bed Chamber and Closet wch opens thro' the house a visto . . . . ye ffloores of ye Roomes are all finely Inlaid, there is very curious Carving over and Round the Chimneypieces and Round the Looking-glasses that are in ye piers between the windows, and fine Carv'd shelves or stands on Each side of ye glass. Every roome is differing work and all fine Carving and over ye Doores some of it is of ye Natural Coullr of ye wood and varnished only—others painted. Ye Duchess's Closet is wainscoated wth ye hollow burnt Japan, and at each corner are piers of Looking glass . . . . The roomes are all painted very finely on ye top.'

The 'neatness' and 'convenience' of smaller houses are also put upon record: 'The House[5] is a halfe Roman H. Ye Hall is in the middle wth double doores, its very lofty and large. . . . .The great hall is divided in half by the staircase wch hangs on its own work not supported on either side to the first half pace and all the way up without support. The other wing of ye House is a large parlour and Drawing Roome; the hall is well painted and a Carved Cornish round and pillars on the wanscoate round the Roome. The parlour is wanscoated and painted a Cedar Coullour'.

Decorative Painting

DECORATIVE painting may be divided into two classes—the covering of the ceiling or walls of a room with compositions in fresco or on canvas, and the productions of decorative pictures, designed to fill the spaces over the door and chimney-piece. The distinction is a convenient one, though the same artists often provided both the large compositions and the small panel pictures. Lanscroon, who painted the staircase and landing at Burley-on-the-Hill, is given £10 15s. for 'two landscapes over the doors in the great parlour',[6] and a painting by Thornhill was used as an overpiece for a chimney-piece at Stoke Edith, where that artist was also at work on the hall and staircase hall (Figs. 57, 58). Many of the state apartments in Hampton Court still have their original overdoor pictures in place. In an old catalogue of pictures bought by George III from the collection of

[1] F. R. Harris, *The Earl of Sandwich*, (1912) vol. i. p. 227. [2] Pearl Finch, *History of Burley-on-the-Hill* (1901), vol. i. p. 71–2. [3] Quoted in E. Colville, *Duchess Sarah*, p. 174. [4] Duke of Marlborough, *Blenheim and its Memories* (*Famous Homes*). [5] Broadlands. [6] 22nd April 1712. Pearl Finch, *History of Burley-on-the-Hill*, p. 70.

Joseph Smith, British Consul at Venice from 1740 to 1760, thirteen of the Canalettos now at Windsor Castle are particularly described as 'Door Pieces'. Sometimes, the large panels of the late seventeenth- and early eighteenth-century wainscot were decorated with a series of paintings, such as the fantastic rocky landscapes in sepia in the hall at Stoke Edith; and Pepys writes of decorative paintings of the royal palaces executed by Hendrick Danckers for himself, the King, and others. The family of de Critz or Cretz had some reputation in the reign of James I and Charles I for decorative paintings, and Evelyn, in 1654, mentions the new dining-room at Wilton, as being 'richly gilded and painted with story', by de Critz.

Of the post-Restoration painters the name of the Italian, Verrio, who is familiar from Pope's couplet, where it is coupled with the Frenchman, Laguerre, displayed the familiar elements of Bolognese decorative traditions. Verrio's[1] first work in England is recorded as being at Lord Arlington's house at Euston before 1671, and he also worked at Montagu House, St George's Hall, Cassiobury, Burleigh and Chatsworth. Among royal commissions he painted at Windsor were the ceilings of the Queen's guard chamber and audience chamber, the King's presence chamber and St George's Hall; at Hampton Court the allegory of the King's great staircase and the King's state bedroom and dining-room. One of his latest works was Queen Anne's drawing-room. Not satisfied with filling in compartments of ceilings, he omitted the divisions as well as the cornice, and often rounded over the angle of the wall and ceiling so that his painting could be spread over the whole surface without apparent break.

Lanscroon, Verrio's assistant at Windsor, worked on his own account at Powis Castle, at Drayton, and at Burley-on-the-Hill.[2] His work on the staircase hall at Arno's Grove, Southgate, of which the subject is the entry of Julius Caesar into Rome, is dated 1723. During the Rochford occupation of Powis Castle from William III's reign to 1722, Lanscroon was employed to paint walls and ceilings in the taste of the day, those on the staircase being 'complimentary to Queen Anne' (Fig. 69).

Laguerre, working a little later than Verrio, does not create so many confused Olympian scenes. As is the case of other decorative painters, much of his work has disappeared with the destruction of the houses he decorated.   In the hall at Blenheim he introduced the motive familiarized by Veronese, of a columnar upper storey enlivened by groups of figures (Fig. 1, frontispiece). At Chatsworth where payment was made to him and his partner Ricard in 1693 and 1694, the quality of his work in the lesser state rooms is remarkable.

The Duke of Montagu, who had leanings to the French style in architecture, invited two French painters, Jacques Rousseau[3] and Charles de la Fosse, to England, who were responsible for the decoration of Montagu House and (probably) of Boughton in Northamptonshire.

Painters working here in the early eighteenth century are nearly all Italians and of the late Venetian school. Pellegrini,[4] who was persuaded by the first Duke of Manchester to try his skill in England, painted the cupola and spandrels of the great hall at Castle Howard. The visits and works of two Riccis (Marco and Sebastiano), the Venetian Belucci, Pietro Damini (a pupil of Pellegrini), the Venetian Amigoni (a pupil of Belucci), are all recorded by Vertue and Walpole. Pellegrini was a facile and inventive decorator; and the reputation he had gained at Venice and Paris recommended him to the Duke of Manchester. Sebastiano Ricci was induced to try his fortune in London by his nephew Marco, who came to England in 1710. He 'met with the most flattering encouragement' in those days of the popularity of the Italian history painter, and painted the chapel at Bulstrode, the hall and some of the ceilings of old Burlington House. The Venetian painter Amiconi, who came to England in 1729 has been described as 'a mere shadow of the old Italian masters, and more feeble even than Sebastiano Ricci', but he found some employment at Moor Park, where he painted subjects 'to place in the hall in lieu of those of Sir James Thornhill, and no doubt intended as a mortification to him'. Thornhill's long

---

[1] 1639–1707.   [2] Gerrard Lanscroon ye painter, for painting the staircase at Burley £150 os. od. For painting the Hall £35. April 23rd, 1712.' Pearl Finch, *History of Burley-on-the-Hill*, p. 70.   [3] Vertue, Note Books, *Walpole Society*, vol. xxii. p. 63.   [4] Vertue, Note Books, *Walpole Society*, vol. xxii. p. 63.

activity lies between the reign of Anne and the first two Georges. He was favoured by Queen Anne and knighted by George I, to whom he was appointed Sergeant Painter in 1720.

Thornhill worked at Windsor and Hampton Court, where the ceiling of the Queen's state bed-chamber (painted in 1716) is by his hand. His surviving work gives some measure of his energy and fecundity. He is both a better colourist and a more competent baroque decorator than his competitors. Thornhill's earliest paintings are at Greenwich Hospital, elaborate compositions in the grand manner, on which he was engaged, from 1708 to 1727. Much of Thornhill's domestic work was perished, such as that at Stoke Edith, Eastbury, Canons, the saloon at Burlington House, and the hall and staircase at Wootton in Buckinghamshire; but he can be sufficiently studied at Blenheim, Chatsworth, Grimsthorpe Castle, and the staircase at Petworth.

The ceiling at Blenheim (which was completed before 1717) is painted with the Duke of Marl-borough, in classic dress, pointing to a plan of the battle of Blenheim, as he kneels to the goddess of Victory. The saloon ceiling also emblematically represents the 'Duke of Marlborough in the career of Victory, arrested by the hand of Peace'. In the Victoria and Albert Museum is a design destined for Blenheim showing Marlborough as Mars, approaching Britannica as mistress of the world on which she is seated. Among his other commissions are a group of houses in Dorset, Charborough and Sherborne House. The work at Charborough, (signed by Thornhill and dated 1718) is the most important in the painter's native county. The architectural features surrounding the painted panels are in *grisaille*. These paintings are well preserved, and show the artist's executive powers, and success in large scale design. There is a fine ceiling painting by him at Grimsthorpe, a late work, as the house was not begun until about 1723.

Every decorative painter of the late seventeenth and early eighteenth century seems to have had a hand in Chatsworth, and Thornhill was not forgotten; the 'Sabine' room, painted soon after 1706, with its complete painted decoration occupying both walls and ceiling is his. At Stoke Edith, Thornhill seems to have worked alone (Figs. 57, 58). In the hall, the projection of the cornice was replaced by architectural relief in perspective, which was a favourite exercise of the painter's ingenuity; while figures from the central group of the assembled gods appeared floating with their clouds beyond the imaginary architectural framework. The lower portion of this two-storeyed hall was panelled, and each large panel decorated in sepia with scenes of fantastic rock-architecture, imaginary towns in impossible situations, which threw up the bright colouring of Thornhill's decorations above. The marriage of Cupid and Psyche appeared on one wall, while on the west wall was an exhaustive gathering of the arts and sciences. The chimney-breast was decorated with a painted figure in a niche with vistas and colonnades on either side. The speaker Foley and other persons were painted looking over a balustrade. The staircase hall represented Apollo and Diana shooting their arrows at the family of Niobe (Fig. 57).

It should be remembered that the rooms treated with the fanciful piling up of statues, porticoes, and balustrades over which figures are leaning, are always passage rooms (such as the hall), or enter-taining rooms (such as the saloon); for the decorator, as in Italy, held any audacity permissible in a room used only by a throng of people, whose mood made them ready to accept the pageants of the walls.

One of Thornhill's latest works is his decoration in monochrome of the staircase walls at Bower House, Havering, which was built in 1729. The lower part of the walls is treated as a masonry base, containing three medallions of allegorical subjects; a pastoral scene, with a shepherd and his flock, decorates the south wall, and on the north wall is painted Silenus and his Bacchic companions.

A sketch-book of Thornhill's in the British Museum shows him as an inventive and accomplished decorator. On the first page is a sepia drawing, with a cartouche inscribed 'jac Thornhill ejus Liber An. Dom. 1699'; and a later sketch is dated March, 1706. A list of subjects from classical mythology and literature is jotted down as suitable for the various walls and ceilings he might be called upon to decorate. There are sketches or measurements of rooms or staircases to be decorated at Easton Neston,

Kiveton, Drayton, and Hewell Hall near Bromsgrove; and there was a sketch at Drakelowe by him of a proposed decoration of the ceiling of the staircase.

In this sketch book he shows a rich execution and a mastery of hand and material quite exceptional in his time. In swelling to heroic size, however, as they covered walls and ceilings, his ideas lost touch with their vivid conception.

Plaster

THE possibilities of modelled plaster (the most plastic of decorative materials and one of the most durable) had been explored in the Tudor and Jacobean periods. The impression given by this plasterwork is intricacy rather than unity of design, but with Inigo Jones, instead of a surface filled with intricate and all-over designs, or ornament contained within small panels, the setting-out became the leading feature, and this setting-out has an emphasized centre. The main lines were simplified; the ceiling was divided by heavy moulded ribs into a few compartments, generally a large central oval, circle or rectangular panel, surrounded by smaller subsidiary panels. The wide soffits of these ribs are enriched with classic detail, such as the guilloche, or by scrolling acanthus, or wreaths of husks, leaves, or closely packed fruits; the sides are moulded and sometimes also modillioned. The centre is left blank as in the ceiling of the saloon and hall at Coleshill, and the porch to the great hall at Kirby. In some cases the central panel was destined for a painting (Figs. 41, 59). In smaller ceilings the central oval panel, as in the porch to the great hall at Kirby, nearly fills the ceiling, and the spandrels are filled with acanthus foliage. The cove has swags and drops, divided by four cartouches. The same setting-out, leaving the centre panel plain, forms the design for ceilings such as that for the 'Cabinett room at Wilton' (1649).

In designs by John Webb, during the Commonwealth, this tradition was carried on, but in some designs there is greater elaboration and ornament, and introduction of acanthus scroll work (Fig. 32). At Forde Abbey, there is something of the indiscriminate wealth of ornamentation of the Jacobean period, and the treatment of the figure subjects is clumsy. At Lamport Hall, it is clear from some remarks in Webb's letters, that the plaster work of the saloon was executed by French artists (much against his inclination), and the character of the ornament supports this.

In the years after the Restoration until the close of the seventeenth century, plaster work moved in the direction of a fresh naturalism in detail in which groupings, festoons, crossed sprays and wreaths of flowers, leaves and fruit were set within a simple geometrical setting of moulded ribs. Birds, *putti* and cherubs are also sometimes introduced. At Denham Place, are two ceilings of unusual character, said to be by Dutch plasterers. In the billiard-room the frieze is in high relief, with painted ornament representing country scenes; the centre of the ceiling is dated 1693. In the coved frieze of the drawing-room, again, various sports are illustrated, and musical instruments and foliage appear on the ceiling (Fig. 61). The ceilings in English houses vary from the intricacy of the Brickwall ceilings (Fig. 60) to the sober effects of the saloon at Melton Constable; for the sole ornament of the smaller, and surrounding the central panel of larger ceilings, a wreath of leaves and flowers is frequently met with. The mouldings surrounding the panels are in most examples enriched with cast or modelled ornament. The units (such as leaves, fruit and flowers) were made separately upon a stalk of strip lead or wire and attached by this stalk to the ceiling. The sharpness and vivacity of this treatment gives the plaster work of this period its interest. During the last quarter of the seventeenth century, the names of a number of plaster workers are recorded. Among them is Edward Gouge[1], who worked at

[1] A design for a room at Coombe Abbey by Gouge (dated 1685) is illustrated in Jourdains' *English Decorative Plasterwork of the Renaissance*, p. 105.

Chatsworth[1] and Coombe Abbey (Figs. 53, 54) and John Grove,[2] who was appointed master plasterer in 1662 and worked for Wren in some of the London churches rebuilt after the great fire, at the Queen's House, Greenwich, and at Greenwich Hospital. Two plasterers, Bradbury and Pettifer, were employed in 1675 and 1676 at Sudbury Hall, on the ceilings of the staircase (Fig. 65), parlour (Fig. 41), and gallery (Fig. 64). Before the close of the century, the naturalistic treatment was less in favour, and Edward Gouge in 1702 complained that for some years past, for want of money occasioned by the war and by the use of ceiling painting, 'the employment which has been my chiefest pretence has been always dwindling away, till now it's just come to nothing'.[3]

Wainscot

PANELLING of the second half of the seventeenth century differs essentially from the small panel style which had been in use throughout the Tudor and Jacobean periods. In this earlier period the subdivision of the surface of the wainscot into small and for the most part rectangular panels was not emphasized; the general plan of the room was often irregular. But in the houses of the new style of building that rose during the Commonwealth, the wainscot had to submit to form part of a decorative scheme. In a transitional room, which was removed from Haynes in Bedfordshire and set up in London, there is no subdivision into panels; the wall surface is divided by Corinthian pilasters of unusual length. The fireplace flank of the room has a pedimented continued chimney-piece as its central feature; on the window side, each window is enclosed in a pillared and pedimented 'tabernacle frame', and a similar frame formed a niche in the centre of the end wall. There are no classical enrichments on the mouldings of the entablature, with the exception of dentil blocks cut out of the solid; but the frieze and soffit are carved with flat arabesques of varied design. The carving of the capitals of the Corinthian capitals is vigorous; and the joinings of the wainscot, which is chiefly of fir, are of close workmanship.

Interiors by Inigo Jones and his school are few; at Coleshill there is no wainscoting dating from the time of its erection and finishing. At Wilton, the double cube room was designed to take the portraits of the Herbert family by Vandyke (Fig. 34). A panel is set out for each picture, enclosing an inner 'lying' panel at the top. Between the panels are drops wrought in composition and applied, the whole scheme being carried out in white and gold.

At Thorpe Hall (1656), Webb's peculiarities, such as his liking for returned and mitred architraves, and other variations upon simpler treatments are noticeable.

In the wainscot of the dining-room of Thorney Abbey House, the large panels are crowned by a cornice. The treatment of some of the panels in the dining-room at Thorpe Hall is very similar. In these examples the panels are recessed, the woodwork is sometimes painted white, and sometimes left in its natural surface. The popularity of pine, which is easily worked, may account for the preference for painted rooms during the years immediately preceding the Restoration. The mouldings are sometimes enriched, and wood carvings, swags, and pendants of fruit and drapery were often applied to salient features of the room.

The wall area was divided into a tall range of vertical panels above a dado. Below the dado, the panels were what was described by Moxon as 'lying', that is, of width greater than their height. The outer edges of the stiles and rails were sometimes enriched with a moulding; and the outer edges of the panels were often bevelled, 'leaving a table in the middle of the panel'.[4]

[1] Account Book of John Whildon, September, 1696, (Chatsworth Library).   [2] See Jourdain, *English Decorative Plasterwork of the Renaissance,* p. 10, 11.   [3] MSS. Earl Cowper, Hist. MSS. Comm. vol. iii. p. 4.   [4] Moxon, *Mechanical Exercises,* 2nd Edition, 1694, p. 106.

The oblong panels were almost invariably large (even 4 and 5 feet in width and correspondingly tall), while smaller panels filled the spaces over the doors and above the fireplace. The panels in the saloon at Erddig, (begun in 1683), are between 5 and 6 feet wide; the panels of the vestry of St. Paul's Cathedral are of small size, necessitated by the small wall spaces and many angles of the room. The mouldings are usually plain, but sometimes an added richness was given by the carving of the door architraves and overdoor and overmantel panels. When exceptional stateliness was desired all the mouldings were carved, as in the Duchess's sitting-rooms at Dalkeith Palace.[1] The most frequent ornament of the frieze and mouldings was the large acanthus leaf, which was a feature of Louis XIV decoration.

There are survivals and records of wood grained and painted. Evelyn gives an instance[2] of the substitution of painted fir for natural oak at Euston, and the fashion seems to have gained ground in the last decade of the seventeenth century, for various houses where the wainscot is painted like marble, or painted a cedar colour, are recorded. At Boughton one state room is painted a shade of drab, and imitations[3] of carved mouldings are stencilled on frieze and cornice. Enriched panelling, where the large panels are separated by fluted pilasters, becomes frequent in the early eighteenth century, at a time when the great height of the rooms, and the absence of the carved adornments would have otherwise given an impression of blank austerity. The fluted Corinthian pilasters are set closely in the wall space, and as a result of the height of the room and the cornice became very ample and many-membered (Fig. 42).

Wood panelling was widely used; not only were all the principal rooms in new houses panelled, but many old houses were fitted with panelling. A noticeable feature is the quality of the joinery known to have been the work of the local craftsmen, even in remote country houses. In such houses timber felled on the estate was used, though for London 'Norway and Dantzig' wainscot was imported; at Kensington Palace the oak used was probably Norwegian, which is richer in grain than English oak. The wood is carefully cut to show as much figure as possible, 'the cuttings being with this distinct object, as nearly as possible radiating from the centre of the trunk of the tree—the medullary rays of the wood being in fact sliced through instead of intersected transversely. This has the effect of displaying the largest amount of the grain.'

The country gentleman was contented with the timber from his estate, but cedar and walnut were also used, as in Trinity College Chapel, Oxford. In Chippenham Hall, near Newmarket, the hall was described as 'wanscoated with walnutt tree, the panels and Rims round wth Mulbery tree yt is a Lemon Coulleur, and ye moldings beyond it round are of a sweete outlandish wood not much differing from Cedar, but of a finer graine'.[4]

Wood-Carving

THERE was a considerable amount of carving to enrich interior woodwork, of a solid, and close style, dating from about 1650 to 1660, without the undercutting, the disengaged details, and the refinements. Swags of carving appear in a chimney-piece at Drayton designed by Webb in 1653, and the woodwork at Tredegar and in the chapel at Farnham; in which heavy, solid swags and drops of fruit form the decoration. The early work, solid and compact, is carved in oak, which does not allow the lightness possible with pine and pear.

The development of joinery after the Restoration is paralleled by that of the wood-carver's art

---

[1] Decorated *circ.* 1703-1709.   [2] *Diary*, 1677. 'The wainscott, being of fir and painted does not please me so well as Spanish oak without paint.'
[3] At Sir Edward Blackett's, the best room was 'painted just like marble' (p. 67) and at Burton Agnes a very good little parlour was 'painted in Veins like marble, dark and white streaks'.   [4]Fiennes, *Through England on a side saddle.* p. 72.

about a decade after the Restoration; and from that date until the end of the century church screens, altar rails, doors to library 'classes', and staircase balustrades are treated with perforated scrollwork, and wainscoted rooms hung with light swags and garlands of flowers.

In smaller places, the decoration of the upper part of the chimney-piece shows the prevalence of the style. The pear-wood carving of military trophies intermingled with oak and bay sprays in the drawing-room of the Governor's house at Chelsea Hospital can be assigned to the William Emmett whose name also appears in the accounts of Windsor, Hampton Court, Kensington Palace, and St. Martin's, Ludgate Hill. Some of the military equipment bears the initials *I.R.* of the last Stuart king. There is no doubt that the carvings of this school were left, 'all white natural wood without varnish', which obscures the tool-work. The recognized *motifs* of this school, 'ffigures, fruitages, beastes, birds, flowers', were used, as a rule, both for the decoration of a country house or a church. The panelling from Winchester College Chapel, (which now forms the decoration at the hall at Hursley) has nothing to proclaim its origin. But now and again subjects were designed especially to illustrate the purpose for which the room was used. In the work of this school there is, in spite of its realism, a feeling for the rhythm and constructive basis of the design.

Nearly all that is known of Gibbons, from his discovery in the reign of Charles II till his death in the reign of George I, may be read in a few entries in the building accounts of the royal palaces, and in Evelyn's Diary. He was given a place in the Board of Works and appointed Master Carver to Charles II, and was employed at Windsor Castle from 1677–1682, also at Whitehall, Kensington Palace and Hampton Court Palace. At Trinity College, Cambridge, Gibbons executed the wreaths of fruit, flowers and arabesques in limewood, with coats of arms of the same material, which enrich the ends of the presses and other portions of the fittings, between March 1691 and March 1693. It seems likely, from the entries in the accounts, that he executed some of the ornamental stonework on the exterior of Hampton Court Palace, besides 'carving cornishes, moldings and picture frames; for architrave, freeze, sub-base and other carvers' worke by him done on and about the sd. Buildings', for which he was paid (1694–1696). In the summer of 1699 he was at work on the limewood enrichments of the King's State Apartments. Later, in the reign of Queen Anne, he was employed (in 1710) in furnishing carvings for the chapel. His carving in the chapel was described as 'the most Exactist workmanship in ye woodcarving, the pattern and masterpiece of all such works'.

Gibbons is most closely associated with Wren; the decorative work at St. Paul's is his, as well as that of several city churches, and his applied limewood carvings in the library of Trinity College, Cambridge. He shows a command of line in his pen-drawings for the ornamental details, such as chimney-pieces, door-cases, etc., at Hampton Court in the Wren portfolio (dated 1694) in the Soane Museum (if these can be attributed to his hand) which are much more florid in character than any actual examples of this school.

The carved work of this school may be divided into complete and isolated decorations, the latter usually consisting of garnitures of chimney-pieces which were not necessarily designed for the position they occupy. The former and more ambitious class is restricted to the Royal Palaces of Hampton and Windsor, and to about half a dozen great houses, such as Cassiobury, Burghley, Chatsworth, Petworth, Belton, Lyme (Fig. 77), and Holme Lacy (Fig. 46). Gibbons, as the designer and carver, is well represented in the Royal Palaces of Windsor and Hampton Court, where he accentuates the features of a room, the overmantel and overdoor and pictures in fixed frames, by his intricate arrangements of ornament. His treatment of the picture varies, and we see it surrounded wholly or only on three sides. His ornament, as in the almost contemporary work at Windsor Castle (1677–1678), is a little tightly packed, the groups, when compared with the carvings of this school formerly at Holme Lacy, at Petworth, and Lyme, are not so skilful and open as the latter. The carvings at Belton are of the same character, and closely resemble those at Cassiobury and Windsor. The most important decoration of this school is found in the immense room at Petworth, part of the additions of the sixth Duke of

Somerset. Here the ornament is arranged about the fixed picture frames; and that about Kneller's portraits of the builder and his wife is a *tour de force*. Each picture is surmounted by the ducal coronet, while the ribbon of the George depends from outspread wings, and below is seen the Star of the Garter. Horace Walpole writes of this room as 'gloriously flounced all round with whole length pictures with much the finest carving of Gibbons that ever my eyes beheld. There are birds absolutely feathered, and two antique vases with bas-relieves as perfect and beautiful as if they were carved by a Grecian master'. He refers again to these vases, one of which he describes as 'an antique vase with a bas-relief of the purest taste and worthy of the Greek age of cameos'.[1] Of the two carved vases, of classical form, one is carved with a procession of Roman soldiers; while the other has a single classical figure within a niche.

The carvings formerly at Holme Lacy (Fig. 46) show a still further advance in lightness and openness of design. The entwined initials, *V.S.J.F.*, which appear in the carving which formerly decorated the saloon chimney-piece, stand for John, the second Viscount, who married Frances, daughter of John, Earl of Exeter, and died in 1697. In the decoration of the saloon at Lyme a still further refinement in design is reached and the arrangement of the ornament in drops of trophies linked by ribbons and trails of leaves, which occupy the centre of the large panels, is not met with elsewhere (Fig. 77). There are six large and two small drops, containing emblems of the four seasons and of music and painting. Of the two small ones, one has the ram's head with an olive branch in its mouth, rising from a ducal coronet, the crest of the Leghs; the other has a group of flowers. Both the trophies of musical instruments and of vases closely resemble those at Petworth. There is no documentary evidence to associate any craftsman with the work, though 'Mr. Gibbons' is mentioned in connexion with 'a peece of carved work' in a letter of 1684, addressed to Richard Legh of Lyme. A panel of dead game, fish, and shells linked by flowers and ropes of beads, in the upper portion of the chimney-piece in the dining-room, reverts to the style of design at Cassiobury and Belton. Late in life he was appointed Master Carver to George I, an office he held under five sovereigns. He died in London in 1720. The work of the younger Edward Pierce,[2] a brilliant carver and sculptor, has only recently been authenticated by accounts and county histories. Plot records his work at Wolseley Hall in Staffordshire;[3] and at Sudbury Hall in the accounts of George Vernon, the staircase carved with acanthus scrolls is entered as his work in 1676 (Fig. 65). Pierce also carved 'the two dore cases on ye top and ye great staires' at Sudbury Hall (Fig. 76). The festoon over the chimney-breast at Coombe Abbey (Fig. 52) corresponds to a pencil sketch bearing Edward Pierce's name.[4] His work is less daring, less complex than Gibbon's known achievements (and than the applied carving at Petworth), though the technique and disposition of the ornament is akin to his.

Chatsworth possesses accounts, in which the date, description, and name of the craftsmen employed in the decoration of the state rooms is given. Chief among the skilled craftsmen was Samuel Watson, a Derbyshire man, who worked, according to his 'Designs, Agreements and Bills of Carved work executed at Chatsworth', from 1690–1712, which gives some idea of the length of time required for such work. In 1692, Lobb, Davis, and Watson agree with the Earl of Devonshire 'to execute in lime-tree the carving of the great chamber, to be done equal to anything of the kind before executed', which shows that the style was established as a standard, and familiar to the English craftsmen. Watson's name is not found in connexion with the decoration of any other house.

[1] Walpole, *Anecdotes of Painting in England*, Ed. Wornum, vol. ii. p. 556.   [2] Edward Pierce died in 1698.   [3] *Natural History of Staffordshire* (1686), p. 383.   [4] *Country Life*, 19th April 1924.

Interior Features

The Staircase—The Chimney-piece—The Door

A CHARACTERISTIC of staircases of the Jacobean period was the massiveness of their parts (the newels, handrail and string). In a few instances during the transitional period the Italian was substituted for the slender Jacobean baluster; and the newels, no longer crowned by a finial, were finished with a moulded cap. The newel itself is panelled, and the string moulded, as at Coleshill and Ashburnham House. At Coleshill, there had to be 'a second or back stair provided to the second story, because the great staires go but to the first story'.[1] Though the staircase runs but from the ground floor to the *piano nobile*, it occupies a large hall with its wide and stately double flights finishing at either end by a landing (Fig. 36). Pierced balustrading instead of the Italian baluster was borrowed from Holland, but carried to greater finish and elaboration here. The balusters of the staircases at Coleshill and Ashburnham House, are of wood, painted white; massive handrails and solid strings were still retained for staircases with foliated balustrades, for the carved work is of great depth[2] (Fig. 69). The scrollwork, which is confined within panels (as at Thorpe Hall (1656) and Eltham (1664), or runs the whole length of the balustrade, as at Tythrop (Fig. 66), consists of acanthus foliations in the midst of which children are sometimes introduced (Fig. 68). The newels have usually a drop of fruit, and are surmounted by a basket, or ornate vase of fruit. At Ham House, which is a variant on this type, the panels are filled with martial trophies of flags, guns, and armour. Similar work is found at Antwerp; in the Brewers' Hall in a staircase of acanthus scrollwork, introducing cherubs' heads.[3] At Forde Abbey (altered in 1658), the staircase panels contain a cartouche from which foliage scrolls repeat on either side. The newel posts, carved with bay leaves, support as finial a vase of flowers. The greater finish and virtuosity of post-Restoration carving is noticeable in later staircases of the same type, as that at Sudbury Hall (Fig. 65) (carved by Edward Pierce), where the acanthus scrollwork of the pierced balustrade repeats on either side of a central cartouche; the deep string is carved with a bay-leaf wreath, and the newel posts are decorated with a drop and surmounted by a basket of fruit. The wall opposite the balustrade is panelled to the corresponding height. After its banishment, the baluster returned to fashion, but with a slenderer shaft, and with its lowest member carved with acanthus. The spiral twist, or 'swash turning' was introduced, and instructions are given by Moxon in his *Mechanical Exercises* (1694)[4] for this enrichment. A balustrade of spirally-turned balusters at Wolseley Hall is combined with the earlier square newel and massive handrail. The practice of 'many modern architects' of placing a twisted rail at the lowermost stair instead of a pedestal is mentioned by Batty Langley in his Builder's *Compleat Assistant*[5] and this innovation becomes the rule in the eighteenth century, with the development of the 'open string', and the shaping of the stair in one continuous curve.

Wrought-iron rails were a feature of the French architecture, and the French smith, Tijou (whose book of designs for ornamental ironwork was published in 1693), exerted an influence over English metal-working. This work gives designs, among other objects, for 'Staircases and panels, of which the most part hath been wrought at the royall building of Hampton Court, and at several persons of qualityes houses in this kingdom'. The design of one 'person of quality's' staircase, can be traced in the balustrade of the stone staircase at Chatsworth. The balustrades were composed generally of long

---

[1] Celia Fiennes, *Through England on a Side Saddle*, p. 18.   [2] Four inches at Eltham Lodge.   [3] Illustrated in Belcher and Macartney, *Later Renaissance Architecture in England*, Fig. 59.   [4] *Mechanical Exercises* (1694) Plate XXV, p. 229–30. ('of. turning swashwork').   [5] *The Builder's Compleat Assistant* (2nd Edition, 1738).

41

vertical panels in early examples, somewhat in the shape of a lyre. With the use of iron balustrading in the last quarter of the seventeenth century, the curved plan becomes more general.

THE CHIMNEY-PIECE

The type of marble chimney-piece designed by Inigo Jones was influenced by Barbet's book on architecture (1633), where the designs have points of resemblance with those at Wilton, where Lord Pembroke was building about 1650 (Figs. 33–35). In what was termed 'continued' chimney-pieces, the lower part in Jones's work is in marble, while the upper part or overpiece of wood, painted and gilt, is a lighter composition. The lower part consisting of an architrave following the forms of Italian door and window openings is complete in itself. Above this architrave is a frieze in which is frequently set a tablet, a feature which may be emphasized by a small pediment. Caryatid terminal figures, and consoles with human heads, and also consoles festooned with fruit, appear as supports. In some instances the chimney-piece projects boldly, and these features are repeated at the sides in profile, as in the double cube room at Wilton. The wooden overpieces, which are of lighter design than the lower stage, are surmounted by a pediment and flanked by columns or pilasters, as in the double cube room (Fig. 34) and colonnade room at Wilton (Fig. 33). The pediment is sometimes broken to receive an armorial cartouche, and the centre of the overpiece is recessed for a picture. This centre panel is usually left blank in the drawings by Inigo Jones and Webb, but in a sketch by Jones for a chimney-piece for the Queen's House, Greenwich, a picture is indicated. With Inigo Jones the frame of the simple chimney-piece and the lower stage of continued chimney-pieces is of white marble, with contrasting dark marble used in some details.

With Webb, the treatment of the chimney-piece remains essentially the same. His effects, however, are gained not so much by form but by contrast and distribution of white and black marble. In an ante-room at Thorpe Hall is a small chimney-piece which is an example of his taste for a pronounced shouldered architrave, which is broken also at the bottom. The spaces between the projections are enriched with a short voluted pilaster. In a small room, or for a simple house, Webb designs chimney-pieces on simple lines with panelled pilasters at the sides, an overpiece consisting of a panel with architrave broken at the top and enriched with short scrolls.

The architects of the half century dating from the Restoration preferred the type in which the chimney-breast was panelled and emphasized as a focus of interest by the addition of a mirror, a picture, or applied carvings. The surround of the opening was a boldly projecting moulding of coloured marble. Genoa was the centre for the exportation of marble, and Evelyn in 1676 tells us that a Dutchman had a large stock of marble and had contracted with the Genoese for all their marble, and set up 'a rare magazine' at Lambeth.[2] The Earl of Rutland, however, a few years later, gets two black and yellow marble mantelpieces direct from Genoa, for which he pays the extravagant sum of £742 7s.[3]

Scagliola was of rare occurrence; but was employed in the Alcove Closet at Ham House in the reign of Charles II, where the chimney-piece and wide hearth slab are made of this material. The design of the chimney-piece consists of scrolls, centring in the cipher and coronet of the Duchess of Lauderdale. The jambs are represented as pillars wreathed with garlands of leaves, and the marble slab has a design of cornucopias, centring in the Duchess's cipher and coronet.

---

[1] From a drawing in the Burlington-Devonshire Collection at the R.I.B.A.   [2] 'To Lambeth, to that rare magazine of marble, to take order for chimney-pieces, etc., for Mr. Godolphin's house. The owner of the works had built himself a pretty dwelling-house; this Dutchman had contracted with the Genoese for all their marble.' *Diary*, 19th September, 1676.   [3] '1683, March 17. Genoa. Account amounting to £742 7s. for two black and yellow marble mantle pieces and two marble stones sent to Sir William Langhorn for the account of the Earl.' MSS. of the Earl of Rutland at Belvoir. Hist. MSS. Comm.

The corner fireplace and the chimney-piece continued as a china-shelf are of Dutch derivation. Evelyn[1] records the innovation in Charles II's new house at Newmarket, where many of the rooms 'had the chimnies in the angles and corners, a mode now introduced by His Majesty, which I do at no hand approve of. I predict it will spoile many noble houses and rooms, if followed. It does onely well in very small and trifling roomes, and takes from the state of greater'. There is a corner fireplace in the King's dining-room at Hampton Court, with two tiers of receding shelves for china or delft. The designs of Daniel Marot are instructive on this point, and one of his chimney-pieces has accommodation for hundreds of pieces of china on its many-tiered continuation. The French architect, D'Aviler,[2] in consideration of the preservation of porcelain, suggests that the height of the cornice of the chimney-piece should be raised 6 feet in order that the vases with which they are ornamented may not be knocked down. The tiered chimney-pieces gained little ground in England. The most usual form has the opening directly surmounted by a mirror, or an arrangement of mirror and picture (Fig. 47). Some of the chimney-pieces at Chatsworth show an arrangement of various shaped panels. In the old state bedroom, the drawing-room and the music-room, the long panel above the opening is surmounted by a shaped panel of parquetry framed in a large enriched moulding which is encircled by applied wood-carving. Even more elaborate carved decorations for the chimney-pieces at Hampton Court are to be seen in the collection of sketches in colour and monochrome in the Wren Portfolio in the Soane Museum, by Grinling Gibbons. A 'continued' chimney-piece was the result, in certain rooms in Dalkeith, of carrying the marble of the surrounds to frame the overmantel panel or panels. A shelf in the modern sense was never used, but a cornice occasionally appears. Marble chimney-pieces with an elliptical arch and key block are characteristic of the late years of the seventeenth and early eighteenth century. This type appears as a lining in the chimney-pieces in the panelled room belonging to John Penhallow in 1686, and removed from 3 Clifford's Inn to the Victoria and Albert Museum. Another type has a plain architrave with projecting corners.

In Vanbrugh's houses the chimney-piece of marble has little ornamentation. A chimney-piece in the hall at Castle Howard stands alone, and may be the work of a French designer. The lower portion is in the architect's massive and plain manner, but the upper is very elaborate with its winged terminal figures and fantastic scrolls.

THE DOOR

In the internal doorways the opening was surrounded by a moulded architrave (frequently shouldered); surmounted by a frieze and cornice. When a monumental effect was aimed at, as in the doorway in the double cube room at Wilton, there are flanking columns and a broken pediment, upon the sides of which figures rest (Fig. 34). Webb's doorways are very varied in detail. In the simple type the shoulder of the architrave is sometimes so exaggerated that it has a pilaster to support it, as in the oak room at Thorpe Hall and the dining-room at Thorney Abbey House. In the doorway in the dining-room in Thorney Abbey House, the architrave is surmounted by a small panel against which on either side short scrolls rest, and above is a cornice. For double doors and doors in more important rooms at Thorpe Hall, Webb shows his inventiveness as a designer. The double door to the library has enriched flanking pilasters, a frieze carved with a scrolling design, and a broken pediment. The door-case in the drawing-room is flanked by carved pilasters rising up above the door to the overdoor, a moulded panel enriched with a bay wreath. In the library the architrave breaks upward in the centre to enclose a small tablet, against which short scrolls rest, and a pendant of fruit hangs down each side of the door-case. A cornice rests on tablet and scrolls, but as if further emphasis were needed, the doorway is flanked by panelled pilasters. No houses dating from the late seventeenth century show so many experimental treatments of the door-case as Thorpe Hall. The door-case with moulded frieze and

[1] *Diary*, 22nd July, 1670.   [2] *Cours d'Architecture*, 1691.

pediment supported by brackets persists, as in the door-case in the dining-room at Canons Ashby. The most widely favoured treatment consisted only of a carved or moulded architrave of bold projection surmounted by carving, or by a picture framed as a panel (Figs. 40–42). The proportion of the door was carefully considered. Gerbier writes that 'the wideness of the door must serve for two to pass at once, that is to say, the doors of Chambers of a pallace', and that the height of a door should be double its width. In other rooms the door should be high enough for a man 'of compleat stature' to pass with a hat on his head.[1] The door was divided into panels of varying sizes. In a few interiors dating from the late seventeenth and early eighteenth centuries, doors were divided into two large panels. The six-panelled door was the most usual. In some of the large doors at Thorpe Hall, Webb introduces an ornament such as a drapery swag or wreath into some panels, but later the panels were left plain. In wainscoted rooms of the post-Restoration period the surrounds of the door and window openings were more closely in touch with the surrounding panelling. The architrave of the door in the late seventeenth century was frequently carved and surmounted either by a framed panel, an overdoor picture or carving, or (less commonly) a bracketed pediment (Figs. 51, 72). The picture or panel, exactly the width of the door, was framed in the same moulding, as the door. When there are many doors in the same apartment, 'the principal ones, provided they stand in the middle of a side or in the middle of the ends of a room, may be larger, of a different form, or more abundantly adorned than the rest'.[2] The ornamental value of a door was recognized; and so much use was made of real and feigned doors that it was objected that these covered so great a part of the walls that no place was left for pictures or furniture.

[1] *Counsel and Advice to all Builders*, London, 1664, pp. 18–19.   [2] *Decorative part of Civil architecture*, ed. Gwilt, 1825, vol. ii. p. 349.

32   Upper stage of the Hall, Lees Court, Kent, *circa* 1652. Showing portion of ceiling with deep moulded ribs
enriched with swags of fruit (destroyed by fire)

33 The Colonnade Room, Wilton House, Wiltshire, *circa* 1650. Chimney-piece by Inigo Jones; painted ceiling by François Clermont, *circa* 1740

34 The Double Cube Room, Wilton House, Wiltshire, by Inigo Jones, *circa* 1650. (The mural decoration in plaster retains its original gilding.). The contemporary ceiling painting by Thomas de Critz

35　The Single Cube Room, Wilton House, Wiltshire, *circa* 1650, by Inigo Jones and John Webb

36 Upper flight of Staircase, Coleshill, Berkshire, with baluster balustrade, 1662, by Sir Roger Pratt

37 The State Bedroom, Powis Castle, Montgomeryshire, *circa 1668*. The woodwork painted, with ornaments gilt

38 The Cedar Room, Warwick Castle, Warwickshire, *circa* 1680

39   The Dining-room, Dunster Castle, Somerset. Dated 1681

40 The Hall of the Strafford Building, Wentworth Castle, Yorkshire, *circa* 1715, a square of 40 feet, with Ionic columns supporting an entablature dividing the ceiling into panels

41　The Parlour, Sudbury Hall, Derbyshire. The Ceiling by Bradbury and Pettifer (1675–76).
Applied carving by Edward Pierce (1676–77). Ceiling painting by Laguerre, *circa* 1690

42   The East Tapestry Room, Wentworth Castle, Yorkshire, *circa* 1715. The chimney-piece flanked by Corinthian pilasters, the frieze enriched by carved consoles

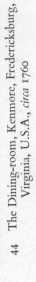

44   The Dining-room, Kenmore, Fredericksburg,
Virginia, U.S.A., *circa* 1760

43   The Tapestry Room, Castle Howard, Yorkshire,
by Sir John Vanbrugh, *circa* 1710

45 The Fourth. Room, Holyrood House, Edinburgh. The wainscoted walls enriched by Corinthian pilasters. Ceiling by Dunsterfield and Halbert, *circa 1674–79*. The blank centre panel framed by a deep border enriched in high relief

46 The Study, Holme Lacy, Herefordshire (before 1694)

47 The Balcony Room, Dyrham Park, Gloucestershire, 1698, by William Talman. The chimney-breast treated with pilasters of the Ionic order; capitals and mouldings and the entablature gilt

48　The King's Dining-room, Drayton House, Northamptonshire. Ceiling and grained panelling
of the late seventeenth century

49　The Tapestry Room, Belton House, Lincolnshire, late seventeenth century. (The hangings bear the arms of
Lord Tyrconnell, dating them after 1718)

50 The Dining-room, Badminton House, Gloucestershire, last years of the seventeenth century. The main doorway flanked by engaged columns, the wainscot divided by fluted pilasters

51   The Billiard Room, Chicheley, Buckinghamshire, *circa* 1715.   System of large panels, interrupted by fluted pilasters, the arch-moulding inlaid with dark and light wood

52   The Drawing-room, Chicheley, Buckinghamshire, *circa* 1715. The panels raised and fielded the applied carvings of limewood. (The chimney-piece not original)

53 Coombe Abbey, Warwickshire, *circa* 1685. Enriched plaster ceiling by Edward Gouge

54 Coombe Abbey, Warwickshire, *circa* 1685, by Captain Wynne. (Both now demolished)

55 Detail of Drawing-room, Marmion, Virginia, U.S.A., *circa* 1735.
The features of the room framed with pilasters. Now installed in the
Metropolitan Museum, New York. (The painted decorations later)

56   The Painted Room, Wilsley House, Cranbrook, Kent, 1685-95

57　The Staircase Hall, Stoke Edith, Herefordshire, *circa* 1710. Mural decoration by
Sir James Thornhill (destroyed by fire)

58   The Hall, Stoke Edith, Herefordshire, *circa* 1710. The upper stage painted by Sir James Thornhill. In the lower stage the
framed panels painted with landscapes in sepia (destroyed by fire)

59 The Drawing-room, Sudbury Hall, Derbyshire. Plaster Ceiling by Bradbury and Pettifer (1675–76). Applied carving by Grinling Gibbons

160   The Staircase Hall, Brickwall, Northiam, Sussex, *circa* 1685. The panels and the ceiling decorated with the Frewen coat of arms and crest, and with floral ornament

61 The Drawing-room, Denham Place, Buckinghamshire, *circa* 1693. The plaster cove decorated with fishing, hunting and shooting scenes

63   The Staircase at 75 Dean Street, Soho. Early eighteenth century
(now demolished)

62   The Staircase, Chicheley, Buckinghamshire, *circa* 1703, with three types of baluster, the
ends of stairs veneered with walnut and their undersides moulded. *Vide* Figs. 72 and 158

64   The Long Gallery, Sudbury Hall, Derbyshire. The ceiling by Bradbury and Pettifer (1675–76)

65　The Staircase, Sudbury Hall, Derbyshire. The balustrade of painted soft wood by Edward Pierce

66 The Staircase, with scroll balustrade, Tythrop House, Oxfordshire, *circa* 1680

67   Scroll Balustrade on the landing

68   Detail of a scroll Balustrade

TYTHROP HOUSE, OXFORDSHIRE, *circa* 1680

69   The Hall and Staircase, Powis Castle, Montgomeryshire. The Staircase with balustrade of enriched
balusters, *circa* 1668. The decoration of walls by Lanscroon, dated 1705

70 The Grand Staircase, Easton Neston, Northamptonshire, 1706, by Nicholas Hawksmoor. The ironwork
balustrade dates from before 1711. Mural decoration by Sir James Thornhill

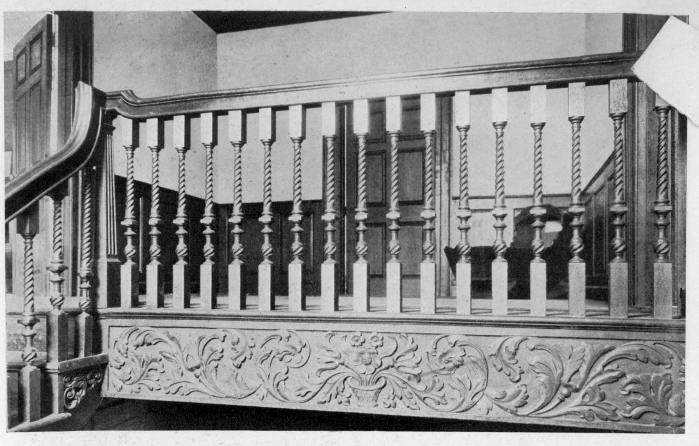

71   Detail of the North Stair with carved fascia, Tuckahoe, Virginia, U.S.A. Built *circa* 1712

72   The Staircase, Chicheley, Buckinghamshire, *circa* 1703

73   The Dining-room, showing pedimented chimney-piece and shelved niche, *circa* 1712

74   The Drawing-room, *circa* 1712. (Now re-erected in the Brooklyn Museum)

CUPOLA HOUSE, NORTH CAROLINA, U.S.A.

76 Doorway at the first floor landing, 1675–76

75 The Queen's Bedroom. The ceiling by Bradbury and Pettifer, 1675–76

SUDBURY HALL, DERBYSHIRE

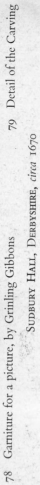

79 Detail of the Carving

78 Garniture for a picture, by Grinling Gibbons

SUDBURY HALL, DERBYSHIRE, *circa* 1670

77 Detail of Carvings in the Saloon, Lyme Park, Cheshire,
circa 1710

81 *Arched doorways, Hope Lodge, Whitemarsh, U.S.A., circa 1723*

80 The Stair and Arch, Sabine Hall, Richmond County, Virginia, U.S.A., *circa* 1730

82 The Dining-room, Easton Neston, Northamptonshire, *circa* 1730. Pictures framed in stucco borders. Ceiling centre probably by Charles Stanley

83   The Hall, Ragley, Warwickshire. The doorways and the scheme of Corinthian pilasters date from
about 1725, the enriched plaster work, *circa* 1755

III

THE EARLY GEORGIAN PERIOD (1720-1770)

Introduction: The Interior

The Palladian School—The Decoration of James Gibbs and William Kent—The French, Gothic and Chinese Tastes—Decoration in America

THE early Georgian style coincides closely with the reigns of the first two Georges and covers the space of forty years between about 1720 and 1760; Defoe's tour leaves an impression of the wealth that had come to the country since the Revolution. It was a great building period 'All the world was mad on building as far as they could reach', as Vanbrugh wrote in 1721, and this limit was often overstepped, since we hear of many who overbuilt themselves and whose houses remained unfinished, or were sold for the sake of their building materials. The age owed a debt to travelled amateurs at a time when a knowledge of architecture was a common accomplishment. Vanbrugh's patrons, the Earl of Manchester and the Duke of Marlborough, showed their interest in the furnishing and building of their houses in their correspondence. Among amateur architects of this period were the Earls of Pembroke and Burlington. Of the ninth Earl of Pembroke[1], Horace Walpole wrote that 'no man had a purer taste in building'. Lord Burlington[2] spent 'large sums in contributing to public works, and was known to choose that the expense should fall on himself rather than that his country should be deprived of some beautiful edifice'.[3] His enthusiasm involved him in debt, and this was also the case with the less magnificent Sir Thomas Robinson[4] of Rokeby, who rebuilt the mansion of Rokeby. There is no design to the credit of Thomas Coke, the first Lord Leicester, who, however, had such a delight and passion for architecture that he frequently discussed the publication of a book of plans of houses from ten to fifty thousand pounds' expense, and some others of less value. This was his favourite study and amusement in the country. Lord Chesterfield spent both his time and money on the building of Chesterfield House. The less famous amateurs had a voice in the building of their houses, for 'in England, more than in any other country, every man would fain be his own architect,' and the result is a very individual and personal quality in great and small English houses.

The reign of George I was the beginning of the spread of the Grand Tour. Before that time it had been restricted to the few; about 1740, as Lady Pomfret writes, it was 'carried a great deal too far amongst the English',[5] and had become a necessity, the usual completion of the education of a gentleman. Thomas Coke was sent at the age of fifteen on his travels, which lasted six years[6]. Lord Burlington his contemporary, spent a considerable time in Italy. Horace Walpole, at the age of twenty-two, went in 1739 to Paris, Rheims, Geneva, Turin, Florence, Rome, Venice, and the south of France. France and Italy were the 'politer parts of Europe' to the travellers, and their stay was generally a prolonged one in the cities of Northern Italy, Venice and Florence. Some of the less carefully conducted young men, as Chesterfield wrote, saw nothing but the English worlds abroad, but in more favourable cases the Grand Tour was so protracted that it is not surprising that the young Englishmen learned something of art and architecture, and developed the habit of collecting pictures, statues, or curiosities. The tour

[1] 1693-1751. [2] 1694-1753. [3] Walpole, *Anecdotes of Painting.* He adds, 'On this account he became so seriously involved in money difficulties that he was compelled to part with a portion of his Irish estates.' [4] 1700-1777. Sir Thomas Robinson travelled over a great part of Europe, giving special attention to the architecture of Greece and Italy, and the school of Palladio. [5] *Hartford and Pomfret Correspondence between 1738 and 1741,* vol. ii. p. 6-7. [6] He returned to England in 1718, having passed through France, Germany, Holland, Flanders, Malta, Sicily, and Italy.

E

was responsible for the formation of the great private collections, which were and are still a feature of the great houses. The Dilettanti Society, a small and private club, was influential in matters of taste from its beginning, though its archaeological work belongs to the latter part of the century. This society, a useful committee of taste, was an adequate board of patronage. Though the Grand Tour included many of the cities of Italy, the influence is Venetian, though the early eighteenth-century Venetian baroque and its excessive floridity was mitigated mainly by English taste. Venice, which held a peculiar position among Italian states, was the 'masque of Italy' and the playground of Europe. It had its industries, its considerable commerce with the East. Here the glass mirrors and chandeliers which were so essential a part of the decoration of the eighteenth-century reception rooms were made; in Venice and in the neighbouring towns velvets and damasks were woven; the carving and gilding of furniture was carried on. Moschini records that the English consuls in Venice were dealers in works of art, and the Republic had taken steps to check the trafficking in antique works of art which were considered as the artistic patrimony of the State. Venice and Vicenza were the richest of all Italian cities in the buildings by Palladio, and a reaction in his favour took place in Italy at the beginning of the eighteenth century due to the writings and propaganda of the Venetian, Fra Carlo Lodoli (1690-1771). The Venetian influence in architecture is consequently marked in England after the early years of George I. Even before Wren's death a reaction had set in. The immediate source of inspiration was the works of Palladio; and more accurate knowledge was rendered possible by the production of Palladian literature. An edition of Palladio was brought out by Leoni in 1715. Campbell's *Vitruvius Britannicus* may be taken as a manifesto of this school, and Palladio was to him the greatest architect the world had known, while Inigo Jones has all Palladio's 'regularity with added beauty and majesty'. But the interior decoration of the English Palladians was not so directly Italian as their architecture. Of the only two architects of this school who had a recognizable and individual style of their own, James Gibbs and William Kent, the decoration of Gibbs can be studied in his published designs and in some of his surviving houses, Ditchley (Fig. 94), the cube room at Sudbrook Park, Petersham and the octagon room at Orleans House, Twickenham (Figs. 95-96). Kent[1] became the 'proper priest' of the Palladian movement. To his circle Palladio 'exceeded all that were before him and surpassed his contemporaries', and Inigo Jones was coupled with him in this admiration. Kent's decoration has a character distinct from contemporary work. He was criticized for his 'constant introduction of pediments and members of architecture over doors and within rooms', and in his wall surfaces he makes use of these elements and also of niches, coffered semi-domes, and consoles carrying busts. . . . A recent enthusiast for his work writes that the hall at Holkham ranks with those of Kedleston and Syon House. There are diverse elements in his interior decoration. He reproduced Roman friezes and actual designs of Inigo Jones and Webb. But there remains much work of his own invention, such as the great hall at Holkham, the 'theatric' staircase at No. 44 Berkeley Square, the Venetian magnificence of some rooms at Houghton (Fig. 84), the Georgian pomp of the cupola room at Kensington Palace. His treatment of simple interiors is to be seen in some rooms of the Treasury.

The taste for collecting objects of art had its influence on the structure of the house. The long gallery had been a feature of earlier house planning, and the gallery or statue gallery is its descendant. At Holkham the gallery was designed for the statues bought in Italy. The pursuit of knowledge had become fashionable. Holkham has both a statue gallery and library; lesser houses were content with a library, with architecturally-designed bookcases or presses ranged along the walls and surmounted by busts or bronzes. The second Earl of Oxford, 'who had no vices, except buying manuscripts and curios

[1] William Kent, (who was born in January 1685-6 and died in 1748) painter, sculptor and architect, was trained in Italy as a painter, and his letters to his patron, Burrell Massingberd, show an appreciation of Italian art. The date of his arrival in Italy is given as 1710; and during his stay in Italy he formed friendships with Thomas Coke and the Earl of Burlington. He returned to London in December 1719, and decorated the cupola room in Kensington Palace in 1721. From 1725 he was given important commissions in the Office of Works. Among his architectural works are Holkham, No. 44 Berkeley Square, the Horse Guards, Devonshire House (now demolished), Wakefield Lodge. See M. Jourdain *The Work of William Kent.*

may be called so', is remembered by the Harleian collection of manuscripts, collected for the most part by him. The great Sunderland Library was housed in the Long Gallery at Blenheim; and at Rousham, General Dormer had an 'incomparable library' in the largest room in the house. Dr. Pococke writes enthusiastically of a box on the Thames, built by a Mr. Bateman, who 'had made what is called a long gallery of three squares; there are books on one side in carved and gilt cases and on the other side they are seen in looking-glass set in like work'. The saloon, which is a feature of houses of the Georgian period, is borrowed from the Italian *salone*, where that room was a ball or gambling room. It was frequently vaulted and often circular in plan, but rarely so high as its Italian original. Architects were constant to the system of an enfilade of reception rooms, opening out of one another and affording 'vistos'. The state apartments were placed by the Palladians on the first floor—the Italian *piano nobile*— which was entered by an exterior staircase which was a feature of the plan. Campbell's description of Wanstead, which he designed, is typical of the arrangement and method of approach of the state apartments in great houses. 'You ascend from the court by double stairs on each side, which land in the portico, and from thence into the great hall, 51 ft. long and 36 ft. wide, and in height the same. This leads into the Salon, being an exact cube of 30 ft., attended with two noble apartments of state all fronting the gardens.' In the villa (called by its owner, by way of contrast, *La Trappe*) 'you were conducted through two rows of antique marble statues, ranged in a gallery floored with the rarest marbles and enriched with columns of granite and lapis lazuli'.[1] A pendant to Cumberland's description occurs in the travels of Dr. Richard Pococke who visited *La Trappe* in 1757, when it had been newly furnished by its owner. 'The gallery which is the length of the house, is a very beautiful piece of architecture of the Ionic order; there is a Venetian window at each end and two windows on each side of an arcade, supported by two fine pillars of Italian marble; in the arcade is a colossal statue of Flora, and in a niche on each side a statue with bronze groups over them. On each side of the arcade and the Venetian windows are busts on terms with bronze groups likewise over. The heads of those at the ends of the rooms are of porphyry. Between the windows are statues, as well as between the looking-glass opposite to the windows. At each end is a column with a vase on them of oriental alabaster and one of the pillars is of the same fineer'd, the other of some very fine marble. The pillars of the door at entrance are of lapis lazuli fineer'd which cost four shillings an ounce. . . . . . The whole is paved with fine marbles in beautiful figures'.[2]   At a country house (Eastbury) there was a 'most magnificent saloon, the whole in stucco, the walls adorned with flowers, etc., gilt, the pediments of the doors supported by pillars all carv'd and gilt, etc., with a Cupid on each side of the pediment, and a bust in the middle where the pediment opens, except at sides where in one is the group of Cupid and Psyche saluting, and that to the garden is an entire pediment with a recumbent angel on each side. . . . .[3]

'On one side are two rooms, one a dining room in which is a beautiful table of fineered Iallo of Siena, with pieces chosen out so as to have a very fine appearance. . . . . The next is the drawing-room, in which on consoles are the twelve Caesars, the heads in bronze, the busts in a kind of agate. The walls of both these rooms, and the ceilings of all of them, are stucco, beautifully adorn'd with flowers and architectonic ornaments gilt, the ceilings being in compartments'.

Wanstead (which was destroyed in 1824) was reckoned one of the finest houses in the kingdom, with nineteen rooms on the principal floor, 'the hall very magnificent, fifty feet high'. 'To look through the suite of apartments has a fine effect; three hundred and sixty feet the length of the house'. Brandenburgh House, at Hammersmith, with its gallery decorated with frescos and gilding and rare marble, was also destroyed about the same date. 'Two of the columns in this gallery were monoliths of Sicilian jasper, seventeen feet high, and the columns of the door case were of lapis lazuli'.[4] Such records give but a partial picture of the great Georgian houses, as the richness of the materials is emphasized at the expense of more essential qualities. The quality of the style depended upon the traditional skill of the

[1] Richard Cumberland, *Memoirs* (ed. 1807), vol. i. p. 185.   [2] *Travels through England*, vol. ii. p. 258.   [3] *Ibid*, vol. ii. p. 139.   [4] *Vitruvius Britannicus*, vol. iv. p. 28–29.

English craftsmen, masons and carpenters, highly trained in the school of Wren and his successors, 'capable of executing the details of Palladian architecture from the roughest indication', so much so that the skill of the English masons was referred to as a matter of common knowledge.

THE FRENCH, GOTHIC AND CHINESE TASTE

Towards the middle of the eighteenth century, apart from the influence of the early Georgian architects, there began to be reckoned with certain fashions, the French, the Chinese and the Gothic. The Gothic is chiefly found in houses where the owners had relations with the literati of the day. This Georgian Gothic had at the time the attraction of novelty, of daring deviation from the classic. Sometimes a whole building, like Strawberry Hill, was conceived and carried out in this style (Figs. 188, 192); and sometimes a single room was treated in the Gothic manner, as the drawing-room at Rousham (Fig. 105) and a bedroom at Claydon.

The Chinese taste offered an alternative to academic classicism; it had never been measured by the five orders. And apart from its revolutionary novelty, there was the attraction of the vividness of colouring in paper hangings, Chinese pictures and lacquer. 'In its predelection for gay and tortuous forms, as also in its love of finish' the art of China was perfectly congruous with Western art. It served to educate the eye and to accustom it to a freer play of line and a more irregular spacing of masses'.[1] It encouraged a tolerance of asymmetry.

The fashion for Chinese decoration has been attributed, though with little foundation, to Sir William Chambers. He was the critic rather than the creator of the movement; and his book was published to be of use to cabinet makers, and 'put a stop to the extraordinary fancies that daily appear under the name of Chinese, though most of them are mere inventions, the rest copies from the lame representations found on porcelain and paper-hangings'. He adds that for the architect the knowledge of Chinese architecture 'is curious, and on particular occasions may likewise prove useful, as he may sometimes be obliged to make Chinese compositions'. At Kew he exploited the Chinese taste on a large scale. He saw that Chinese architecture did not suit European purposes, but he also realized the charm of the occasional use of Chinese interior decoration. Its principal characteristics are the use of open lattice-work or frets as bordering to the wall-papers, and the introduction of Chinese *motifs*—such as pagoda roofs, Chinese birds, figures, and bells—into the woodwork. A correspondent in the *World* (1753) takes credit for the fact that Chinese ornaments were 'not only of our own manufacture, but of our own invention'. Its place was in inferior rooms (according to Sir William Chambers); in 'rooms of pleasure' (according to Ware). In the Chinese room at Claydon—which is the fullest expression of the Chinese vogue—everything is Anglo-Chinese. The decorator, one Lightfoot, was at work here in 1768–9.[2] The immense alcove for the bed is a wilderness of rococo, with a background of lattice-work. The niches were originally designed to contain 'mandarins and pagods, and twenty things from China that are no use in the world', such as Goldsmith's lady of fashion collected; and the present Chinese figures look very well as a substitute. The pagoda-like shape and the bells that dangle from every point are in the Chinese tradition. The great width of the alcove is a curious feature, and may have been designed for a 'bed of uncommon size', such as found a place in Bubb Dodington's 'Managareth' (or the Chinese bedroom) at Eastbury which was described by a contemporary as 'excessively droll and pretty, furnished exactly as in China'. The dissemination of the taste by means of pattern books carried it to America, and in the *Carolina Gazette* (1757)[3] a house is advertised for sale 'new built . . . . after the Chinese taste'. The staircases of 'Chinese paling' in England and the United States are surviving examples of large-scale frets (Figs. 111–113).

The vogue of the rococo (or French taste) invaded England shortly before 1740 and lasted for

---

[1] Allen, *Tides in English Taste*, p. 234. [2] *Architectural Review*, vol. lx. p. 50. [3] Quoted in Waterman, *Mansions of Virginia*, p. 52.

over a score of years. The earliest published designs in this style are those of Gaetano Brunetti, who in 1736 brought out a book of designs 'very useful to painters, sculptors, stone-carvers, wood carvers and silversmiths'. The characteristic of the style was a combination of flamboyant and restless motifs pierced and convoluted shells and rockworks, stalactites and short scrolls which could be extended without any continuity of design (Figs. 90, 98, 114, 118).

As Lord Burlington was the leader of the classical style, Lord Chesterfield (whose own Grand Tour did not extend to Italy), identified himself with the French taste, and expressed it in Chesterfield House, which was 'to be furnished *a la Francaise*'. The house was designed by Isaac Ware, and Lord Chesterfield took possession of it in 1749, writing in that year that he had 'yet finished nothing but my boudoir and my library; the former, the gayest, and most cheerful room in England, the latter best'. Of the library, he writes, in 1747, 'that the ceiling is done and most of the wainscot is up. The bookcases go no higher than the dressings of the doors, and my poets, which I hang over them, will be in stucco allegorical frames, painted white'. The poets, in rococo frames, were surmounted by an inscription from Horace, which extended round the room in foot-long capitals, beneath the cornice. There was no gilding in the room, the constant fire and candles would 'so soon turn it black, whereas by having it new painted once in four or five years it will always be clean and cheerful'. Lord Chesterfield expected some opposition to his entirely French house, and, writing to his friend Bristowe, says: 'I think you will like it, but whether you will dare to own it I am not sure, considering that the *schola* fulminates so strongly against it'. An exceptional rococo scheme of decoration existed in a house at Painswick in which the enriched mouldings and the chimney piece are classical, but the ornaments on the ceiling and walls are rococo.

DECORATION IN AMERICA

The ideal of the Colonial style in America 'remained always conformity to current English usage',[1] and this close similarity can be accounted for by the wide circulation of architectural publications and builders' handbooks. It has been possible to identify the book from which certain forms, doorways, chimney-pieces, staircases, flanks of rooms and details of ornament used in American houses were derived. The interior of Carters Grove shows throughout parallels to the plates of *Palladio Londonensis*. A chimney-piece in the mahogany room in the Lee House, Marblehead, follows line for line a plate in Abraham Swan's *British Architect* (1745), which contains a great variety of 'new and curious chimney-pieces'. A characteristic of American interiors between about 1725 to 1760 was the employment of niches or alcoves or of enclosed cupboards with arched beads (Figs. 100, 102, 104).

Wooden panelling was commoner during the first half of the eighteenth century[2] than after 1750, and this decrease in woodwork was related to the vogue for paper hangings. It is not uncommon for a panelled room to be enriched by an order of pilasters. The parlour at Marmion is treated by an order of Ionic pilasters flanking all the features and supporting a full entablature (Figs. 55, 102).

---

[1] Fiske Kimball, *American Domestic Architecture*, p. 150. [2] *Ibid*, p. 116.

Decorative Painting

Kent—Amiconi—Casali—Clermont

DURING Thornhill's lifetime pictorial scene-painting went out of fashion; and the ceiling decorations were restricted to painted panels within a setting of stucco. The walls (with the exception of the walls of hall or staircase) were no longer painted, and even the hall and staircase walls were treated in monochrome with conventional arabesques (or 'grotesques' as they were called), or with the representation of statuary in niches. Kent's experiments in a style hitherto untried in this country are to be seen in the smoking-room at Rousham, and in the presence chamber at Kensington Palace. He designed ceilings composed of arabesque ornaments in the style of Raphael's Loggie in the Vatican. It has been stated that these paintings were in imitation of those 'then recently discovered on the ruined walls of Herculaneum and Pompeii', but these were not disinterred until after the ceilings in the presence chamber and the smoking-room at Rousham were decorated. The plaster behind the cornice of the former bears the date 1724; the colours are bright reds and blues, enriched with gilding. These ceilings, warm in colour, attractive in design, were fitted for the enrichment of a low room. Kent's own 'inventions' often fill the central panels in the ceiling, while the subsidiary panels have monochrome decoration representing vases, emblems, and trophies reminiscent of Roman mosaics. His paintings at Esher and Wanstead are no longer in existence, but he can be judged by his work at Kensington Palace and the hall at Stowe. A Venetian painter, Sleter, adopted Kent's 'mosaic' manner in his treatment of the immense coved ceiling of the state dining-room at Stowe, and he was also employed on decorative work at Mereworth. Kent also embraced in his practice the older school of allegorical painting, but these paintings, which formerly extended over walls and coved ceiling, were restricted in extent, and disposed in compartments and panels. His talents as a painter was not commensurate with his success, which he owed to the ardent patronage of the architect Earl of Burlington. Among his works is a series of paintings in the King's Gallery at Kensington Palace, representing the story of Ulysses; and a central cubject, Mars and Minerva, with a figure of Painting at their feet and emblems of the other arts, in Queen Caroline's drawing room in the same palace. The grand staircase at Kensington Palace, where Kent attempts the massing of human figures in the Venetian manner, is unique in his work. The upper part of the north wall of the staircase hall and the north end of the east wall is painted with a gallery, with its balustrade thronged with a medley of courtiers, pages and servants, yeomen of the guard, together with a curious creature, 'Peter the Wild Boy' brought to England in 1726. Round the landing are feigned niches, painted in monochrome with figures of Apollo, Diana and Hercules. The ceiling has four painted segments on three of which musicians are depicted, while on the fourth Kent has introduced his own portrait, with two of his pupils. The decoration did not please George Vertue, who speaks of it as 'poor stuff . . . . a terrible glaring show'.

The names of two Italian painters, the Venetian, Amiconi, and Andrea Casali occur during the middle years of the century. Amiconi, who is mentioned as having lately arrived in England in 1730, painted at Moor Park, where his work was 'in lieu of those Sir James Thornhill did', and at Powys House, Ormond Street, where the painted staircase hall is described by Vertue as in 'the light and pleasant manner of the Venetian'.[1]

Andrea Casali (who worked in England from about 1741[2] to 1766), painted scenes from Roman history for the saloon at Wanstead, and at Fonthill. Among his surviving decorations are panels in the octagon room at Asgill House, Richmond, painted with gods and goddesses in colour on a bistre ground, and the dome of the Staircase Hall at Hovingham Hall in Yorkshire.

[1] Vertue, *Note Books, Walpole Society*, vol. xxii. p. 67.   [2] *Ibid*, p. 58.

There is no instance of the decoration known as *Singeries*, covering both the walls and ceiling; but the French painter, François Clermont[1] painted the ceiling of a small building on Monkey Island at Bray, 'with monkeys fishing and shooting'. Clermont, according to Horace Walpole, 'painted in grotesque, foliages, with birds and monkeys, and executed several ceilings and ornaments of buildings in gardens; particularly a gallery for Frederick, Prince of Wales at Kew; two temples in the Duke of Marlborough's island near Windsor (called from his grotesques Monkey Island), the ceiling of Lord Radnor's gallery and of my Gothic Library at Twickenham .... and a ceiling for Lord Northumberland at Syon'.

Lord Baltimore's villa, called Belvedere, on the Thames, contained 'two small parlours, in one, panels painted of monkeys, another scaramouches, which the old Lord Baltimore used to call "Monkey and Scaramouch parlours".' A monkey parlour, in which the ceiling has a lively decoration of monkeys, was painted in 1745 for Kirtlington. The large oblong centre panel has a rayed head in the centre and a light decoration of birds and floral devices, while the cove is devoted to *singeries*, the monkeys in appropriate costume riding upon hounds and hunting the fox, the deer, and the hare.

Plasterwork

The Palladian School of Plasterwork—The Italian Stucco Workers—The Rococo

DURING the early eighteenth century, a simplified French style was general, and in ceilings the decoration was often limited to a broad margin with rounded or incurved angles. In the period of Italian influence, when stuccoed walls were almost universal in great houses, Palladian architects relied upon 'the ancients', to whom Inigo Jones was added as of equal authority. At Holkham a Roman frieze was reproduced in the great hall, and the ceiling was adapted from a design by Inigo Jones.

Much of the ornament of contemporary design was the work of Italian *stuccatore* who combined competence in the modelling of figures with a wealth of undistinguished detail. Gibbs speaks of two of them, Artari and Bagutti, as 'the best fret workers that ever came to England'. Albert Artari, 'gentleman plasterer' worked at Houghton (where the ceiling and the frieze of boys in the Stone hall are by him), at Sutton Scarsdale (in 1724), at Canons and at Ditchley. Bagutti was responsible for the stucco work at Mereworth (which was finished in 1725) at Canons, and for a ceiling at Canonbury. Francis Vessali (or Vossali) shared the stucco work at Ditchley with an Italian, Charles Serena. Two Italian stucco workers, the brothers Paul and Philip Franchini, who introduced the use of modelled stucco in Ireland, worked chiefly in Dublin; but the decoration of the staircase hall at No. 15 Queen's Square, Bath, is attributed to them. The bas-relief treatment of the figure of St. Cecilia, and the contest of Apollo and Marsyas is characteristic of the art of the Italian stucco worker (Fig. 108).

The penetration of the *rocaille*, a style embodied by France in the lovely elegance of the Régence, is later in England, but it had become 'the fashionable distemper' in 1740. The characteristic of the English version of the style is a combination of flowers and leaves, pieced by tattered shells and rockwork, and short scrolls which could be readily adapted and extended. Long festoons and drops of flowers and trophies of musical instruments (Fig. 124), symbols of sport and rustic life, a variant upon the rococo, appear in the dining room at Easton Neston (Fig. 82) and the saloon at Hagley Hall (Fig. 91).

Cast medallions were often introduced among the rococo ornament, as in a room at Clandon Park, and in the Whistlejacket room at Wentworth Woodhouse (Fig. 90).

[1] Clermont returned to France in 1745. Paintings in gouache are preserved at Alnwick. See M. Jourdain, *Country Life*, 7th December 1929.

Wainscot

Niches and Alcoves

NATURAL wood panelling almost entirely disappeared with the accession of George I, and where it reappears, as at Houghton,[1] it is the new and expensive mahogany that is used, and not oak. When wainscot appears, its colour and surface are disguised with paint or graining. Deal or pine, which were both cheap and easy to work, had taken the place of oak by the middle of the eighteenth century, and, as all carved work was painted and gilt, one kind of wood did as well as another; Ware speaks of it as 'almost the universal timber'. The flank of the wall was arranged in a system of wide, or of wide and narrow panels. In Hogarth's print of the *Industrious Apprentice advanced to be Sheriff of London*, the wall shows an arrangement of wide, divided by narrow, panels. In the large panels pictures are hung, while the narrow panels contain an ornamental drop. The overdoor panel and that above the chimney-piece were still the appropriate places for pictures, and when Walpole was building Strawberry Hill, Horace Mann sent him from Italy a set of *sopra porta* pictures. Rooms 'in the most elegant buildings' (according to Ware) were finished with ovolo and plain panels in the broad margins[2]. The panels were recessed, and the moulding left plain or ornamented with classic detail. The recession of the panels and the delicacy of the mouldings and their ornament, is an example of the return of the early Georgian architects to the style of Inigo Jones. Excellent examples of this style of panelling are Kent's work in the smoking-room at Rousham, which has wide and narrow recessed panels.

Applied carving was very much less in favour with the Palladian architects, as was natural with their preference for stucco; but at Marble Hill, Twickenham, there is carved applied woodwork of eagles supporting swags of foliage above the large panels of the saloon, and the overdoor enrichment of two amorini supporting a basket of flowers above a mask and swags of foliage, the lion's mask and oak-leaf swags between the windows of the same room (Fig. 123).

About the middle of the eighteenth century a certain amount of woodwork was used, showing French influence in its light, floral ornament, of which the house at Painswick was an example. Of the later rococo, allied with Chinese *motifs*, the alcove in the Chinese bedroom at Claydon is an illustration; but the ornament of this class was concentrated upon the chimney-piece and the door-case, leaving the walls free.

NICHES AND ALCOVES

A feature of the early years of the eighteenth century is the shelved recess or cupboard framed on the wainscot. Such recesses were often surmounted by a semi-hemispherical head (Fig. 188), often fluted, painted, or carved with a shell; and the pilasters framing the recess in the finer examples break up the monotony of the plain wall surface. In a richly treated alcove from Bristol, the shelves are supported by pierced and carved brackets.

With the decay of interior wood work in the late eighteenth century these built-in niches disappeared, and they had already become less frequent by the middle years of the century when walls were hung with silk or paper hangings.

---

[1] Built between 1722 and 1735.   [2] *Complete Body of Architecture* (1756), p. 739.

84   The Marble Parlour, Houghton Hall, Norfolk, by William Kent, *circa* 1731. The panel in the upper stage of the **chimney-piece** by Rysbrack. The whole of the side, including the alcove and sideboards, of marble

85 The Saloon, Holkham Hall, Norfolk, by William Kent (after 1734). The frieze and the octagon panels
of the cove copied from Roman originals

86   The Saloon of the Provost's Lodge, Trinity College, Dublin, 1760, by John Smith.
(After the designs by Richard, Earl of Burlington)

87 The Shell Grotto, Goodwood House, Sussex, *circa* 1730

88   The Low Drawing-room (originally Dining-room), Wentworth Woodhouse, Yorkshire, *circa* 1740

89   The Tapestry Room, Hagley Hall, Worcestershire. The painted ceiling panels by James Stuart, *circa* 1758

90 The Whistle-Jacket Room, Wentworth Woodhouse, Yorkshire, mid-eighteenth century. Ceiling and walls decorated with rococo plasterwork

91   The Saloon, now the Dining-room, Hagley Hall, Worcestershire, 1758. Plasterwork by Vassali

92   The Gallery, Hagley Hall, Worcestershire, *circa* 1758

93 The Entrance Hall, Hagley Hall, Worcestershire, *circa* 1758. (Plasterwork by Vassali)

94   The Hall, Ditchley, Oxfordshire, *circa* 1722, by James Gibbs

95 The Octagon Room, Orleans House, Twickenham, *circa* 1720, by James Gibbs

96   The ceiling of the Octagon Room, Orleans House, Twickenham, *circa* 1720

98 Ceiling on the first floor, House of Charity, Soho Square, London, mid-eighteenth century

97 Ceiling of the Hall, Ragley Hall, Warwickshire, *circa 1755*

99 The Drawing-room, Brandon, Prince George County, Virginia, U.S.A., 1765–70, walls panelled, and chimney-piece with large overmantel panel framed by an architrave and pediment

100 The Palladian Room, Gunston Hall, Fairfax County, Virginia, 1755–58 (the interior the work of William Buckland, an English joiner), the windows and niche framed by pilasters

101 Waterman House, Rhode Island, U.S.A., *circa* 1785

102 The Drawing-room, Marmion, Virginia, U.S.A., *circa* 1735. All the features of the room framed with pilasters
(installed in the Metropolitan Museum, New York)

103 Staircase and arch, Jerathmael Bower's House, Somerset, Massachusetts, 1770

104 Flank of a wall in North East Parlour, John Brown House, Providence, Rhode Island, U.S.A., 1786. Joseph Brown, architect

105   The Drawing-room (formerly the Library), Rousham, Oxfordshire.
The stucco framework of the pictures by Roberts of Oxford, 1764

106   The Staircase, Ragley Hall, Warwickshire. Staircase, *circa* 1725

.107 Hall and Staircase, 9 Henrietta Street, Dublin, 1731. Probably by Richard Cassel

108   Upper storey of Staircase Hall, 15 Queen's Square, Bath, *circa* 1728. John Wood, Senior, Architect. Plaster by Franchini brothers. (Staircase now removed)

109   The Entrance Hall, Carter's Grove, Virginia, U.S.A., 1751–53, showing staircase and arch

110   Main stairway, landing and windows, Benjamin Hall Junior House, Medford, U.S.A., *circa* 1760

111 Detail of Staircase at first landing, Battersea,
Virginia, U.S.A., 1765–70

112 "Chinese" Staircase, Boughton House,
Northamptonshire. Mid-eighteenth century

113 The Stair Hall, second floor. Bohemia, Cecil County, Maryland, U.S.A., 1743–45

114 Chimney-piece in the Hall, Ragley Hall, Warwickshire, *circa* 1755. Stucco panel, *circa* 1755.
System of Corinthian pilasters and entablature are 1725

116 The Fireplace in the Front Room, 31 Old Burlington Street,
London, *circa* 1735

115 The Fireplace in the Library, Crichel House, Dorset, *circa* 1730

118   A door in the Tapestry Room, Hagley Hall, Worcestershire, *circa* 1758

117   The doorway in the Entrance Hall, Easton Neston, Northamptonshire, *circa* 1702, by Nicholas Hawksmoor

120, 121   Two doorways in the Front Room, 31 Old Burlington Street,
London, circa 1735

119   A door in the Gallery, Hagley Hall,
Worcestershire, circa 1758

124 Plaster ornamentation in the Drawing-
room, Hagley Hall, Worcestershire,
circa 1758, by Vassali

122 Carving in the Library, Ragley Hall, Warwickshire

123 Carved and gilt applied Ornament in the Saloon at Marble Hill, Twickenham, *circa 1725*

125   The Anteroom, Syon House, Isleworth, *circa* 1762–65, by Robert Adam.
The gilded stucco wall panels by Joseph Rose

Interior Features

The Staircase—The Chimney-piece—The Door

THE eighteenth century is the period of the curved plan; the handrail, and the newel, as was natural in the curved plan, lost its importance, and the string is generally open. The intersecting angles of the straight rails at the landings were suppressed, and the balustrade was shaped into a continuous flowing curve. The change in the planning of houses accounts for the fluctuation in size and treatment of the staircase. The Elizabethan and Jacobean staircase led from the ground to the upper floors where the long gallery and the great chamber were situated. With the Palladian treatment of the ground floor as the basement, when the first floor became the Italian *piano nobile* reached by an external flight of steps, the grand staircase had to be sacrificed, though variations in planning (and especially the exigencies of a town site) prevented its entire disappearance. In the case of Devonshire House, built on a roomier site, when the external staircase was removed in the middle of the nineteenth century, a new staircase had to be built within doors. The typical Palladian staircase did not run beyond the first floor, as the course to the floor beyond would render the height of the well disproportionate to the walls, and this moderate height was especially necessary when the ceiling was to be painted or otherwise decorated. When Blenheim was building, it was recorded as a novelty that there were only 'a little pair that goes to the upper rooms'. The Italian baluster, as used at Coleshill (Fig. 36), was adopted by the Palladians instead of the group of two or three balusters for each tread which was in more general use. Examples of this Palladian staircase are those of 30 Old Burlington Street and of Marble Hill, Twickenham (the latter built in 1724). The closed string in both cases is carved; and the newel posts at Marble Hill are enriched with ornament in their panels. The group of balusters was capable of variations in design.

Staircase Ironwork. *From* Welldon's '*The Smith's Right Hand*', 1756.

These were taller and more slender than the type usual in the late years of the seventeenth century, and were generally set three to a step. The ornament of the walls and ceiling of the staircase was considered, for, 'there is no part of a house where the eye is more naturally directed upwards than the staircase. When we enter a room the variety of objects calls the eye from place to place, and the furniture as well as the decoration claims this undivided attention, but in passing upstairs the eye is naturally directed to the sides and top, and this justifies the finishings usually bestowed upon these parts of an edifice'.[1] The walls of the staircase hall were painted or ornamented with plaster (Figs. 107, 108). The

[1] *Complete Body of Architecture* (1756), p. 48.

53

F

taste for large painted compositions disappeared before the middle of the century, and wells and halls were treated with plaster ornament.

In America, during the colonial period, stairs had been composed of straight runs of steps; but shortly before the Revolution, a tendency appears to curve the landings, using winders to affect the curve.

THE CHIMNEY-PIECE

The architects of the early Georgian period went back to Inigo Jones 'the first who arrived at any great degree of perfection in this material branch of the art'[1] of designing chimney-pieces as their model, and designed in his manner. In the architectural publications of the eighteenth century, the character, material and ornament are treated. *The Chimney-piece maker's Daily Assistant* (1766) gives a table showing 'the true size that chimney-piece ought to be' for the various sized rooms. They may be roughly divided into (1) the architrave type, or (2) those with trussed pilasters, (3) caryatid or terminal supports, or columns to support the mantel-shelf. Kent uses a scroll-shape side and frontal console in the chimney-piece in the marble parlour at Houghton (Fig. 84), the side console in the White drawing-room and the frontal console in the Cabinet-room. At Holkham the dining-room chimney-pieces have a frontal console. Ripley carries on this type of chimney-piece at Wolterton, where the chimney-piece in the White Hall is doubly buttressed with consoles. This type is not favoured by Gibbs in the chimney-pieces that figure in his drawings and in his published work; which are considerably lighter than those of Kent, and built up on classic lines.

Chimney-pieces were made of one or two storeys; or, to adopt Ware's term, were of the simple or continued type. The former defined a chimney-piece which terminated at its cornice, or by a pediment or other such ornament over it. The different styles of treatment of the 'simple' and the 'continued' chimney-pieces are dealt with very fully by him.

The simple chimney-piece was thought better suited for rooms hung with paper or silk or treated with simple mural ornament (Figs. 92, 114); consequently the velvet-hung saloon at Holkham, though a large and important room, has chimney-pieces of this type (Fig. 88). The continued chimney-pieces have an upper structure of stucco or of wood, which continues, though it forms no part of, the lower structure of marble, and contains a picture or a sculptured panel (Figs. 90, 94). The upper portion is crowned by an open pediment which is often broken to receive a bust, or other decoration.[2] Ware suggests that the blank space in the panel of a continued chimney-piece could be filled with a wind-indicating dial. He even gives an illustration of his idea with the dial surrounded by scrollwork and 'four cherubims puffing at the cardinal points'. The continued chimney-piece was the more important, but neither kind was ever treated by the architects as an isolated detail, but as part of, and indeed the keynote to, the decoration; and Ware condemns the young architect whose chimney-piece does not correspond to his overdoors.

Among sculptors who carved chimney-pieces during this period were Peter Scheemaker and John Michael Rysbrack. Chimney-pieces by Scheemaker are recorded in the green velvet bedchamber and the green damask drawing-room at Ditchley,[3] and by Rysbrack[4] in the marble parlour at Houghton (Fig. 84).

The stay of a third Flemish sculptor, Laurent Delvaux[5] in England was brief, but he appears to have kept up a connexion with England after he returned to the continent. An account (dated 1767) gives particulars of his 'carving and polishing the head, carving the husks on the face of the marble and jambs, and polishing the ground' of a chimney-piece at Nostell.[6]

A fourth sculptor of this period was Sir Henry Cheere,[7] well-known for his large practice in supplying monuments, garden figures and architectural accessories. There are chimney-pieces by him

[1] *Decorative part of Civil Architecture* (ed. Gwilt, 1825), vol. ii. p. 370. [2] 'The pediment should be open, because it will then receive a figure'. Ware, *Complete Body of Architecture*, 1756, p. 563. [3] *The English Connoisseur* (1767), vol. i. p. 33. [4] Rysbrack came to England from Antwerp, and died in London in 1770. [5] 1695–1778. [6] Brockwell (M) *The Nostell Collection*. [7] 1703–1781. He was created a baronet in 1766.

at Ditchley and at Wallington Hall. His brother, John Cheere, was also a figure-maker and probably a painter. His name appears in Mortimer's *Directory* in 1763 as established at Hyde Park corner.

There were also 'many ingenious and very able sculptors, of whom one chief employment is to execute magnificent chimney-pieces, now happily in vogue'. The result of Chambers's innovations was that chimney-pieces were also made by manufacturers, and sold like furniture to the owners of houses, rather than designed by the architect to suit the character and proportions. According to the architect and antiquary, John Carter, many of the principal chimney-pieces and monuments of that day issued from the firm of Carter. The subjects of the sculptures on the frieze on the tablet were always considered, and suited to the character of the room.

A vine-wreathed head or Bacchic *motifs* were frequently found in dining-rooms, and when symbolism was not required 'no ornament (according to Ware) was so fit as a head'. During the middle years of the eighteenth century, subjects were drawn from Aesop's *Fables*.

Chimney-pieces were made of marble and wood, but only marble—white or coloured—was used 'in high-finished apartments'. When a combination of white and coloured marble was used, the ornament was of white, while the plain portions, such as the grounds of the frieze and the tablet and the shafts of the columns, were of coloured marble. Variegated marbles were considered as best suited to the simple, and plain to the continued types. At Holkham, in the two saloon chimney-pieces, the columns and ground of the frieze are sienna marble; in the dining-room the consoles and ground of the frieze are of Sicilian jasper; against these grounds, 'festoons of flowers, trophies and foliages, frets and other decorations cut in white statuary marble have a very good effect'. Ware gives an exhaustive list of the plain and variegated marbles from Italy, Spain, Egypt, Devonshire, and elsewhere in use in England.

So large was the supply of English chimney-pieces that it is rare to find one imported from Italy. Through all the marble chimney-pieces of the Georgian period there will be observed a continuous classical tradition, and departures from this style expressed themselves in other materials—the revived Gothic, in stone; and the version of the French rococo style, in wood. The latter was designed not by architects like Chambers, but by 'upholders' and cabinetmakers. All but one of Abraham Swan's designs for chimney-pieces are rococo. The wooden chimney-piece, like the panelling of the day, was not left in its natural colour, but the prevailing shades of green, cream, light blue, and brown were used.

The rococo style began to prevail about 1740, and was applied at first to the ornament, the old lines being retained, but later 'the scrolls and inverted C's' broke through the outline as wildly as in contemporary designs for mirror frames. The style reached its greatest extravagance in combination with the Chinese taste after the middle year of the century.

THE DOOR

With the Palladian architects the pedimented door-case which becomes the rule rather than the exception in important rooms, has a solid and imposing appearance with its large enriched mouldings (Figs. 86, 94, 95). Between the architrave of the door and the pediment there was a frieze, of which the most usual pattern was the pulvinated, ornamented with ribboned oak or bay leaf. But scroll designs in carved and gilt wood, often centring in a shell or lion's head, or a classical mask, are also met with. The pediment, if broken, was often filled by a bronze or plaster bust (Fig. 85).

IV

THE CLASSICAL REVIVAL OF THE LATER EIGHTEENTH CENTURY (1760-1820)

Introduction: The Interior

The Age of Collections—The Work of Robert Adam—Sir William Chambers—The Classical Revival

THE long reign of George III falls into two well-marked divisions, on either side of the barrier of the French War. The personal influence of the King, whose reign is taken as the bounds of this late Georgian period, counted for little, though he had the reputation of taking an interest in art, especially architecture. In the earlier half from the Peace of Paris until Pitt's declaration of war on France in 1793 the industrial revolution began to mature, and national wealth was heaped up from the textile, iron, and mining industries. At this period, owing to the riches which flowed into the country after the Peace, houses rose 'like exhalations'. In the second period following the French Revolution, England was locked in a struggle which could never have been carried to its end without the amassed wealth of the years of peace. It was only in the first period that unimpeded travel on the Continent was possible; within two years, from the peace of 1763, no less than forty thousand English had passed through Calais; and when France sided with belligerent America, Walpole was able to say that though at war with France neither country took much notice of it. The small class that enjoyed the monopoly of political power consisted, down to the French Revolution, of men who were accustomed to draw pleasure and profit from Italian galleries and French salons, and liked to surround themselves with sculpture from Rome and with Venetian pictures that recalled the liveliest hours of the grand tour, or with the scattered treasures of a foreign library or collection of medals and gems. It was generally recognized that the foreign tour was a training in the arts and the art of living. 'Some young men of distinction are found to travel through Europe', writes Goldsmith, 'with no other interest than that of understanding and collecting pictures, studying seals, and describing statues'.

Many houses had their sculpture or picture gallery. The collectors of the reign of George III were not the slaves of a single school; for Dutch, Flemish, and French pictures were also all shipped to these shores. Such amassed and accessible wealth set the standard of accomplishment in architecture and decoration, and of a clientèle of critical patrons, which can only be estimated by those who compare them with the country gentlemen of the early eighteenth century as described by Fielding, and with a later generation when this cosmopolitan education was a thing of the past, and the interest of the owner in the building and decoration of his house is evidenced by tradition, by the individual quality of the work, and by the preservation in many cases of the architect's sketches, and the owner's memoranda.

In a small private society of gentlemen which for more than a century and a half exercised a considerable influence in the fine arts, and whose enterprise in the field of classical excavation and research is memorable, this taste for classical antiquities was encouraged. 'The foundation of the Dilettanti Society brought together all the rich young travellers of British birth in a kind of healthy competition towards one single goal. Under the spur of this competition, purses were opened freely, and with the help of English gold the soil of Rome and the Campagna yielded up its long buried treasures'.[1] To the Society belonged for a long period the chief, and in some instances the sole, credit of initiating and supporting undertakings by which the remains of classical antiquity in Greece and the Levant were explored, surveyed, and published. In France, in spite of the zeal of a Caylus or a Cochin, little share was taken in the work of research until after the Revolution.

During the late seventeenth and early eighteenth century, the Arundel and Pembroke Collections stood alone in England. 'A few excellent copies of the antique in bronze or plaster were admitted as single embellishments of the palaces of our nobility, but the more frequent ornament of libraries and saloons were busts by modern sculptors'. Dallaway, à propos of the rarity of classical sculpture in England, tells a story of 'a gentleman of one of the western counties' who had bought two capital antique statues in marble at Rome; had brought them to England and placed them in his garden. His son and successor was not a virtuoso and had married a city lady addicted to fashionable improvements. She directed these ill-fated marbles to be painted, in order, as she observed, 'that they might look like lead'.[2] William Kent and the younger Matthew Brettingham were commissioned to procure antique statuary for Holkham, and Sir Robert Walpole had collected several busts and heads by means of Brettingham for his house of Houghton; but such collections were, until the later part of the century, exceptional. The rapid growth of collections of statuary can be estimated by the Dilettanti Society's publication in 1808 of the *Select Specimens of Ancient Sculpture preserved in the Several Collections of Great Britain*, which illustrates, besides Payne Knight's and Towneley's collections, specimens from the galleries of Lord Lansdowne, Lord Egremont, Mr. Hope of Deepdene, Lord Yarborough, and Lord Cork. To the credit of the Englishmen of this period these collections were often freely lent for reproduction. No circumstance has tended so much to improve the national style of design and painting as the introduction of so many genuine antiques or correct copies of them. Over five hundred owners of gems were laid under contribution by Tassie in forming his series of reproductions, and several collections were open to Josiah Wedgwood by his patrons. The first attempt to make a collection of casts from the antique for the use of the public dates from 1758, when the Duke of Richmond, returning from his tour in Italy, opened to the public his paintings, sculptures, and casts, gathered in a gallery in the garden of his house at Whitehall, as a gratuitous school of drawing.

Charles Towneley, who had for many years his headquarters at Rome brought with him, on his return to London in 1772, a vast collection, and in his town house in Park Street (now Queen Anne's Gate) he exhibited his stores of Greek and Roman art with accompaniments so admirably selected 'that the interior of a Roman villa might be suspected in our metropolis'. He is represented by Zoffany in an inner hall lighted by a skylight, seated amidst a welter of statues, surrounded with marble figures, sepulchral tablets, cinerary urns, sarcophagi, bas-reliefs, columns, winged creatures, busts, and the like, spoils he had gathered in Rome when the contents of Hadrian's Villa were dispersed. To Sir William Hamilton, a member of the Dilettanti, who was for thirty years Minister Plenipotentiary at the Court of Naples, the nation owes a great part of its collection of Greek and Roman antiquities. He used his influence to interest the Court of Naples in the Pompeiian discoveries, of which he published an account; and was one of the first Englishmen who collected and appreciated Greek vases. He had the ambition, he writes, 'on continuing as long as I am able, to do everything in my power for the advancement of the fine arts, particularly of those in my own Country', and collected antiquities both for their own sake and 'the profit which I thought modern artists might reap from them'.[3] He generously circulated the proof plates of his collection,[4] which were drawn upon as a source for Wedgwood's Etruscan vases[5] and also for the Etruscan style in which Robert Adam experimented. In a letter to Wedgwood, in 1773, he promises him some 'drawings of fine shaped vases', and begs him to continue 'very attentive to the simplicity and elegance of the forms, which is the chief article'.[6] His first collection

[1] Cust and Colvin, *History of the Society of the Dilettanti*, 1914, p. 124.   [2] *Anecdotes of the Arts in England*, London, 1800, pp. 269–270,   [3] Preface, *Recueil de gravures d'apres les vases antiques tirés du cabinet de M. Hamilton*, vol. i. Naples, 1791.   [4] *Antiquités Etrusques grecques et Romaines tirées du cabinet de M. Hamilton*. Naples, 1766–1767.   [5] Wedgwood in 1769 writes that he is 'preparing to paint the vases after Mr. Hamilton's book', *Letters to Bentley* (1762–1772), p. 279.   [6] E. Meteyard, *Wedgwood and his works*, vol. i. p. 49.

was bought by a vote by the nation in 1772, and so great was the demand for Wedgwood's imitations that it was said that their sale amounted to two years in the sum paid for the originals. Hamilton continued collecting, and Goethe in 1787 found his vaults at Naples full of busts, torsos, vases, and bronzes. Some of this second collection passed into the collection of Thomas Hope of Deepdene. Among travelled collectors of the last years of the eighteenth or early nineteenth century may be mentioned Richard Payne Knight, the 'arbiter of fashionable virtu', who joined the Dilettanti Society in 1781, and collected chiefly bronzes, coins, and gems; Sir Richard Worsley, British Resident at Venice, who explored Greece and the islands and coast of Asia Minor in 1785-1786, and formed a large collection which he brought home; and the Wiltshire antiquary, Sir Richard Colt Hoare.

Another group of persons who shared the taste for classical antiquity was the colony of English artists and connoisseurs who made Rome—the centre of the trade in real and manufactured antiques—their headquarters. Among these were Jenkins the banker and Gavin Hamilton the painter, who is remembered chiefly for his remarkable excavations in Italy, and who helped to form the Lansdowne Collection. Jenkins (the banker) supplied foreign visitors with intaglios and cameos, made by his own people, that he kept 'in a part of the ruins of the Coliseum fitted up for them to work slyly by themselves'. This production of spurious antiquities at Rome was animadverted on by Dr. Clarke, who accompanied Lord Berwick on his tour, and found a 'system of imposition and villainy practised here upon poor John Bull every hour of the day. The greatest of these Romans carried cheating to such a degree of ingenuity that it becomes a science, but in baking legs, arms, and noses they really surpass belief'.

Georgian art is pervaded by an extraordinary and unusual finish and refinement; it inclines to a certain coldness and arrogance of expression, its very perfection of taste lending it 'a certain exclusiveness as of a thing aloof from common appreciation, and of too delicate an order to be understood by the vulgar'.[1] It is, in short, in all respects aristocratic. It was by men of such informed taste—virtuosi—artists and architects, that the classic reaction was fostered. The descriptions published by the *Accademia Ercolanese*[2] of the buried city in 1757, a few years after excavations began on the site of Pompeii, the new interest in Greek architecture and antiquities dating from Le Roy and 'Athenian' Stuart's publications, the influence of writings of Winckelmann, the engravings of Piranesi, combined to effect a revolution in taste. In 1754 Le Roy visited the East, and four years afterwards appeared his *Ruines des plus beaux Monuments de la Grèce*. The huge *Recueil d'antiquités égyptiennes, grecques, gauloises* of the widely travelled Comte de Caylus began to appear in 1754, and five years later in his *Tableaux tirés d'Homere et de Virgile*, he gave a collection of subjects for painters and sculptors. By the middle of the century, classical archæology was no longer a learned speciality but an interest of the cultured world. That a Greek revival in architecture was introduced immediately was not the case, though ornamental detail was slightly affected, and in 1762 architects had little to guide them but Le Roy and the first volume of Stuart and Revett's *Antiquities of Athens*. It has been said that on the appearance of this volume 'there was a great sensation among the admirers of the fine arts, it grew into a mania for Greek architecture',[3] and that the 'Grecian gusto', (as it was called) was fashionable among the Dilettanti Society. But the Greek revival was, in fact, delayed for a generation after the first volume of the *Antiquities of Athens*; and though Stuart reproduced the anthemium and fret of the Greeks, his characteristic decoration, such as in the boudoir and bedroom at Spencer House, is of the Italian arabesque type. It is impossible to reconcile the statement that Stuart and Revett found themselves 'elevated to the position of fashionable architects in a new but sadly inadequate application of the classical style to domestic use'[4] with the really negligible quantity of their output. The prime mover in the architecture and decoration of the second half of the eighteenth century was not Athenian Stuart but Robert Adam.[5]

[1] *Contemporary Review*, August 1911. [2] Herculaneum was first excavated in 1711, and excavations were renewed in 1738, and continued until 1766. In the discovery of the *Villa dei papiri* in 1754 the climax was reached, and 'a vast number of antique bronze utensils that were found, furnished a glimpse of the wealth of beautiful form with which the handicrafts adorned the whole life of an ancient city'. The excavations were abandoned in 1766, and Pompeii, accidentally discovered in 1748, took its place in interest. [3] Mulvany, *Life of Gandon* (1846), p. 197. [4] Cust and Colvin, *History of the Society of the Dilettanti*, 1914, p. 81. [5] For a full study of the life and work of Adam see James Lees-Milne, *The Age of Adam*, 1948.

It is possible to point to certain elements, such as Italian fifteenth-century decorative painting, the vast archæological repertory furnished by Piranesi, as conditioning the delicate decoration by Robert Adam. These influences are slight; and what overweighs them is the rich fertility of Adam's design. He set his mark upon decoration from the accession of George III until his own death in 1792. From about 1772 his style was generally adopted by younger men, such as James Wyatt, Thomas Leverton, and the younger Dance, and some of the older Palladians, and it is now a matter of some difficulty to distinguish between the work of Adam and that of his imitators. Of the work of Sir Robert Taylor, an older contemporary, there is little left but the interior of the Court Room of the Bank of England (Fig. 164), and Ely House, Dover Street. Sir William Chambers, a learned architect and a fine draughtsman, might have been expected to form a school. His sketches are brilliant and vivid in handling; he kept a record of French and Italian detail and had made notes of English Palladian detail; he spent infinite pains upon the choice of his assistant artists and workmen, and remarked that 'the most masterly disposition incorrectly executed can only be considered a sketch in painting or an excellent piece of music murdered by village fiddlers', and his work bears evidence that he never lost sight of this principle. He had models made for his Ionic, Composite and Corinthian capitals from the finest Roman originals, and he was entirely convinced that his decorations approached 'nearer to the most approved style of the ancients than that of the Adams'.[1] Chambers had studied in Paris, and there is in his architecture evidence of the influence of contemporary French work, as, for instance, of Gabriel. He also follows the French tradition in ornamental detail, in his use of foliage and flowers, and this introduction of the natural forms of leaves and flowers is shown in his designs. His time was, however, much occupied by designing triumphal arches and casinos, and by the great work of his life, Somerset House; and his output of domestic work was relatively small. He saw with dismay the first beginnings of the Greek revival, and maintained that architectural knowledge ought not to be collected from the remains of Grecian buildings, but from 'some more abundant source, which, in whatever relates to the ornamental part of the art, can be no other than the Roman antiquities'.[2] Hence his sympathy with the Palladian style which, 'though somewhat heavy, was great, calculated to strike at the instant, and although the ornaments were not so varied or numerous as now, they had a more powerful effect . . . they were easily perceptible without a microscope and could not be mistaken for filigrane toy-work'.

The style of Adam, when he returned from Italy in 1758, was not completely formed. His early work still shows the influence of the Anglo-Palladian school, as in the ceiling (1759) for Admiral Boscawen at Hatchlands. Yet even at this early date he is conscious of a mission and is convinced of 'the confusion and littleness of the present style, and the simplicity and elegance of the ancient manner'. His earlier ornament as we see it in the drawing-room ceiling at Kedleston is large in scale, little removed from the undistinguished contemporary florid design. It is only his matured work, not the tentative essays at Shardeloes and Kedleston, that is illustrated in his *Works*, which exhibit a formed coherent style.

The completeness of the revolution in taste effected by Adam is referred to by Gandon, and by Sir John Soane, who, in a lecture to the students of the Royal Academy, describes the routing of the rococo ornamentation: 'This taste soon became general; everything was Adamitic, buildings and furniture of every description'. The new treatment was adopted as being truer to the interior design of Greek and Roman houses than the Palladian tradition. Adam developed a style in which the mouldings were smaller and slighter, and the painted and stucco ornament was drawn from the Italian Renaissance grotesques, which were themselves derived from Roman fresco painters. The fact that discoveries at Herculaneum 'testify that a light and fantastic architecture of a very Indian air made a common decoration of private apartments'[3]; must have struck every traveller to the buried cities. The diary of James

[1] *R.I.B.A. Journal*, 24th August 1893.　[2] *Decorative Part of Civil Architecture*, ed. J. Papworth, 1835, p. 79.　[3] *Anecdotes of Painting in England*, ed. Dallaway and Wornum, vol. iii. p. 58.

Adam shows him intent upon copying such decorations in Italian villas as would prove useful. In the Villa Petraio, at Florence, he admires 'a considerable collection of porcelain and plates, with grotesque ornaments, infinitely pretty, and well worth copying'.[1] At the Villa Castello also he notes that 'there are many of the rooms painted in the grotesque taste with spirit and invention, also the ceilings of several of the rooms are done in imitation of treillage work, with vines twisting round them'. At the Palazzo Vecchio, 'the apartments of this palace are full of grotesque ornaments, but of a kind superior to any I ever saw, which made me form the project of employing a young painter to copy most of them for me during my absence'. Throughout their practice, the Adam brothers kept in close touch with Italy, and kept modellers at Rome employed in copying bas-reliefs and ornament for them. Among the younger contemporaries of Robert Adam whose decorative work has affinities with his are James Wyatt and Thomas Leverton.

The full tide of Wyatt's success may be dated from the completion of the Pantheon in Oxford Street, and it was the fashion to consider him more 'chaste' than Robert Adam. He was in favour with George III, who considered him the first architect in the kingdom.[2] His painted decorations, as at Heveningham (Fig. 136), were entrusted to Italian artists, with whose methods he must have been well acquainted during his long years of study in Rome and Venice, his ornament as expressed in the library ceiling at Belton, and his sketches for ceiling and mural decoration in the Victoria and Albert Museum are thin and wiry. Wyatt's later work, such as Dodington, Gloucestershire, became more severe and monumental (Figs. 133, 149, 154, 160, 162). Leverton, the controlling influence in the design and decoration of Bedford Square, avoids Wyatt's bare and linear treatment. His ornament resembles that of Robert Adam, but its detail is extremely minute; and he shows a preference for enriching linear forms with delicate and lace-like detail, and a freer use of naturalistic forms, as in the stucco of the chimney breast of the dining-room at No. 1 Bedford Square. He has an individual and playful treatment of classic details that can be traced in the interior of Woodhall Park, where acorns alternate with dentils in the doorhead, and his Bedford Square houses, where diminutive Doric columns are suspended by their capitals to the lowest member of a cornice.

With the death of Robert Adam in 1792 and the opening of the Twenty Years' War with France in 1793 marking the close of a period, the cosmopolitan atmosphere among the English patrons of art came to an end. The importation of works of art from Italy ceased in the last decade of the eighteenth century, and the agents settled in Rome died or disappeared. From this moment dates England's severance from the Continent, and with it the rise of an aristocracy as insular as any of their countrymen.

Decorative Painters and Designers of Ornament

THE baroque decorative painting of the late seventeenth and early eighteenth century had completely fallen from favour by the middle years of the eighteenth century; Horace Walpole, writing in 1760 of Chatsworth, speaks of the inside as most sumptuous, 'but it did not please: the heathen gods, goddesses, Christian virtues, and allegoric gentle folks are crowded into every room as if Mrs. Holman had been in heaven and invited everybody she saw'.[3] The English *Singeries* and *Chinoiseries* decorations have not the sparkle and finish of the *Singeries* and *Chinoiseries* in France, though carried out here by the French artists. Interiors were decorated with the modelled plaster rather than with brushwork until after the middle years of the eighteenth century were passed, and Sir William Chambers speaks of the total absence of decorative painting at this time, 'for one cannot suffer to go by so high a name the trifling gaudy ceilings, now in fashion, which,

[1] *Library of the Fine Arts* (1831), vol. ii. pp. 9, 10. [2] *The Farington Diary*, 1794. [3] *Letters*, ed. Toynbee, vol. iv. p. 423.

composed as they are of little rounds, squares, hexagons and ovals, excite no other idea than that of a dessert upon the plates of which are dished out bad copies of indifferent antiques'.[1] Large decorative paintings covering the whole expanse of the ceiling were, in Adam's view, misplaced and tiring to the eye, for 'great compositions should be placed so as to be viewed with ease'[2]. He therefore invariably preferred Renaissance arabesques or subjects on a small scale filling the lunettes, circles, squares, and oval compartments of his ceilings (Figs. 130, 152), and the preference for such painted interiors is evident after about 1770, in the work of Adam, Chambers and Wyatt. The majority of the artists who carried out this decoration were foreigners; such as the Italians Zucchi, Cipriani and Bonomi; and the Swiss, Angelica Kauffmann. In certain cases the panels were painted by the artist himself, as is evidenced by accounts, but a design was repeated by the many minor artists; the central medallion of the Judgment of Paris by Angelica Kauffman in the drawing-room ceiling of No. 1 Bedford Square is also used on the ceiling of a back room in No. 10 of the same Square, together with the replicas of the smaller painted panels. Of the popularity of such paintings, George Richardson's *Iconology*, with its numerous emblematical designs and its large list of subscribers, is sufficient evidence. The book aimed at providing artists with 'the most effective means of rendering the ornaments that adorn the sides and ceilings of the apartments of the great expressive and significant;' so that decorations could be suited to the client.

Angelica Kauffmann (1741–1807) is the most widely known of these painters. From her arrival in London in 1766, her popularity was marked; for a few years after she had exhibited in the Royal Academy for the first time Allan Ramsay observed that 'Cipriani himself was not more admired'. Her pictures have all the superficial qualities of the classical movement in decoration; she developed what has been called the sentimentality of the antique, with a fluid and uncertain grace, mannered, but with a certain decorative quality. Four paintings on the ceiling of the vestibule at Burlington House, signed medallions in the back parlour at Chandos House, and the ballroom ceiling at Stratford House, are by her hand. The decorative paintings in 20 Portman Square, designed by Adam for Lady Home in 1773, and the ceiling paintings of the music-room of No. 20 St. James's Square are attributed to her. At Syon House, the medallions on the library ceiling (which was designed by Adam in 1762), a mosaic of octagons and small diamonds, are ascribed to her, but these bear a close resemblance to emblems of Richardson's *Iconology*. Antonio Zucchi (1726–1795) was a very competent artist. His work is effective in colour and composition, and is highly finished. He painted the fixed pictures of scenery and buildings in the music-room at Harewood House, panels in the dining-room ceiling at Kedleston, and two rooms at Saltram. The ceiling of the drawing-room at Newby was (according to a description written in 1789) by Zucchi. The subjects of Zucchi's segmental panels for the dining-room at Saltram—Plato teaching his pupils, Virgil reading the Æneid, Alexander the Great and Aristotle, Anacreon sacrificing to the Graces, and the monochrome medallion heads of Thales, Zeno, Socrates, and Cicero—are an indication that the room was originally designed for a library; but in 1781, when Zucchi was paid, it was termed the 'eating-room'.[3] The centre of the saloon ceiling is also by him. He figures very prominently in the correspondence with Sir Rowland Winn for the decoration at Nostell; the tapestry-room ceiling at Nostell is probably by him.[4] The paintings on the ceiling of the Library, Kenwood, are also by him.

Among the Italian group of Adam's assistants, the Florentine Cipriani, who came to England in 1755 with Sir William Chambers, was responsible for much decoration during his thirty years' stay in this country. He painted panels for the anteroom of Lansdowne House, compartments in the coves of the library allotted to the Royal Academy in Somerset House in 1780; and the ceiling of the ballroom of Melbourne House, Piccadilly. The ceiling of the library at Buckland was designed by him and carried out by him and Rebecca. It is an imposing allegorical design, representing an open dome

[1] *Decorative Part of Civil Architecture* (ed. Gwilt) 1825, vol. ii. p. 398.   [2] 'The rage of painting became so prevalent in Italy that instead of following those great examples, they covered every ceiling with large fresco compositions, which though extremely fine and well painted were very much misplaced, and must necessarily from the altitude in which they are beheld, tire the patience of every spectator.' *Works in Architecture* vol. i. p. 4.
[3] Entry in Mr. Parker's MS. account book (1781), 'Zucchi for paintings in the eating-room'.   [4] M. Brockwell, *The Nostell Collection*, p. 15.

wherein figures representing the arts and sciences, poetry and history appear among clouds, shepherded by Apollo and Minerva. He was 'excellent as a draughtsman, but his style of colouring in oil pictures was rather cold and sometimes hard'.

Biagio Rebecca (1735–1808) who was also long resident here, worked at Windsor in the state apartments, and with Italian facility he would 'paint you a history piece, a ceiling, or a peep-show picture' (Fig. 163) with equal readiness. He was employed by Sir William Chambers at Somerset House, by Robert Adam and by James Wyatt. At Heveningham the arabesque decoration of the saloon is his work, and ceiling, walls and door panels, and even the chimney-piece are invaded by his light Pompeian fantasies lightly brushed in. In 1794 he was paid for work at Lichfield House, No. 15 in St. James's Square.[1] The ceiling paintings of the gallery at Harewood House (Fig. 152) are attributed to Rebecca, and he painted the Pompeian room at Audley End. Among the native decorative painters of this period are William Hamilton (1751–1801), who painted arabesque and ornaments in the style of Zucchi, and John Hamilton Mortimer, who painted a ceiling at Brocket Hall.

Chiaroscuro or grisaille painted upon a grey or coloured background was occasionally used instead of fully coloured panels and medallions. De Gree, a painter from Antwerp who painted in Ireland, made a speciality of work 'in imitation of basso-rilievo'[2] with great effect. The work of painters of the late eighteenth century was criticized by contemporaries for the smallness of its scale and weakness; and Horace Walpole speaks of artists as 'too feeble to paint anything but fan-mounts'.

As an alternative to the small panel picture framed in stucco, arabesque design in the manner of the Renaissance was carried to its culmination in the latter part of the eighteenth century. The fact that arabesque ornaments and figures in any situation are perceived with a glance and require little examination, made them, in Adam's view, better adapted to ceiling decoration than the complexities of large compositions. James Stuart, a painter rather than architect, 'with his usual elegance and taste contributed greatly towards introducing the true style of antique decoration', and light animated arabesque treatment of walls may be seen in the music-room at Stowe and at Heveningham. Of the painter of the Stowe arabesques, the Italian, Valdré, little seems to be known. The central panel of the ceiling has the dance of the Hours and Seasons round the Sun, and the large wall panels are painted with delicate finish and vivacity. Motifs drawn from vase paintings or Pompeian wall decoration were used as decoration during the late years of the eighteenth and early nineteenth century. The cupola-room at Heaton Park has similar arabesques on walls and ceiling; over the chimney-piece is a draped medallion supported by two veiled sphinxes; and above this again is a painted fan; the walls are divided by arabesqued pilasters, and the dome has grisaille arabesque panels on a brown ground. A late survival of arabesques in a small room at Southill, having lunettes over the doors, and the light, fugitive painting on the ceiling.

A name hitherto unknown among decorative painters is that of Julius Cæsar Ibbetson,[3] a landscape, marine and figure painter, whose unfinished wall decoration is preserved in the drawing-room at Kenwood. His scheme as it stands consists of terra-cotta coloured panel borders, enlivened by small oval medallions, of which the subjects are children sporting, scenes of country and (an innovation very characteristic of the date) industrial life, dated sketches (1796) for which are preserved at Kenwood. The large panels are blank, but there is no doubt that they were to be filled in, as one shows the beginnings of a group of *amorini*.

A short-lived fashion about the last decade of the eighteenth century was that for panoramas, or seeming continuations of an extensive view, examples of which may be seen at Norbury, near Leatherhead, and in a room formerly at Drakelowe, which is attributed to Paul Sandby. Of the latter house,

---

[1] 1794. Biagio Rebecca—'To painting four oval pictures for the drawing-room ceiling at £12 12s.
    2 oblong Pictures for drawing-room ceiling at £5 5s.
    4 round Pictures in bas-relief.
    4 round Pictures in colours.' MS. accounts of Lichfield House.

[2] Mulvany's *Life of Gandon*, p. 215. [3] 1759–1817.

Miss Seward writes: 'Sir Nigel hath adorned one of his rooms with singular happiness. It is large, one side painted with forest scenery, whose majestic trees arch over the coved ceiling; through them we see glades, tufted banks, and ascending walks in perspective. The opposite side of the room exhibits a Peak Valley, the front shows a prospect of more distant country; real pales, painted green and placed a few inches from the walls, increase the power of that deception.' This curious *trompe-l'œil* has been removed to the Victoria and Albert Museum; a rival panorama projected at Chatsworth in 1790 by the Duchess of Devonshire was ruthlessly checked by the Duke, who hastened down to Derbyshire, and dismissed all the panoramic artists on the spot, much to the displeasure of the Duchess. The Norbury drawing-room, painted, it is said, by Barrett, Cipriani, Gilpin and Pastorini with landscapes, intended as seeming continuation of the view without, was much praised by Gilpin in his *Observations on Picturesque Beauty*.

Walls were sometimes hung with pictures of regulated sizes, symmetrically disposed; as in the dining-room at Kedleston, Saltram and at Heaton Park. These essentially decorative pictures were often painted for the space they were to fill, and were uniform in subject. 'If a picture', Gilpin writes, 'does not please at sight, it is fitter for a painter's chamber, or a curious cabinet, than for a saloon or a drawing-room'. Pictures of the late Italian school were the favourite 'furniture pictures', and not only were genuine Panninis and Canalettos imported, but English painters imitated them successfully. A painter of lanscapes, Harding, according to Vertue, was constantly imitating paintings of Canaletto of Venice, and also paintings of Pannini, with good success. Decorative landscapes with small figures in the style of Zucarelli had become popular, and Zucarelli himself twice visited England, his second stay extending from 1752 to 1773. He exhibited landscapes with figures at the Royal Academy in 1769 and 1770. Zucchi, to judge by the subjects of his pictures exhibited at the Academy between 1770 and 1779, adopted Zucarelli's style, and painted large landscapes with classical buildings, and figures dancing or sacrificing.[1] The fixed pictures are usually framed in a margin enriched with transverse fluting, between two sets of mouldings, with angle pateras or rosettes, but occasionally the more important paintings are more richly framed.

Among the Italian ornamentists and decorators was Michele Angelo Pergolesi, who published engravings at intervals between 1777 and 1792, which include designs for plate, panels for painted or stucco arabesques, repetitive ornament of a delicate and graceful character, and compositions in which the centres of *amorini* and sporting children are engraved after Cipriani by Bartolozzi, friezes, and chimney-pieces. In the original prospectus he states that he has designed and painted rooms, ceilings, and staircases, and ornaments for the nobility and gentry of England and other countries, and in the first Duchess of Northumberland's *Book of Prices of some of the work done at Syon* is a note 'Sixty two pilasters by Pergolesi at three guineas each', which probably refers to the painted pilasters on the long gallery. Collections of his original sketches are extant. Ninety-six of his original drawings of arabesque ornament are entered in Quaritch's General Catalogue for 1883, and a correspondent in *Notes and Queries*, in 1882, writes of a large folio volume of coloured drawings in his possession, lettered on the back 'Pergolesi's Drawings from Montfaucon', all signed, and dated 1776. The date of Pergolesi's death is not known, but in 1801 his successor, Duluchamp, speaks of the late Signor Pergolesi.

George Richardson,[2] an admirable engraver, was an assistant in the office of the Adam brothers, by whom he was employed in drawing and designing for eighteen years. He exhibited at the Royal Academy and the Society of Artists of Great Britain, and published besides the *New Vitruvius Britannicus* which illustrates houses and public buildings erected during the last quarter of the eighteenth century, designs for chimney-pieces, ceilings, and vases and tripods; and *Iconology*[3], a collection of emblems for the use of decorative painters, plasterers, and sculptors. He dedicates his book of *Ceilings* to Lord

[1] 1770 Ruins of a monument at Sibaris. 1771. A ruin of an ancient monument, with figures dancing. 1778. The remains of an ancient building, with figures in Oriental dress. 1779. The remains of an ancient temple of Ceres, with figures representing a sacrifice to the gods.
[2] 1736?–1817? [3] *Iconology*, 1779, 2 vols.

Scarsdale, and the last plate illustrates the ceiling of the hall at Kedleston. The front room of No. 32 St. Stephen's Green, Dublin, was carried out from Richardson's design, which also appears in his book of *Ceilings*[1] as executed for Lord de Montalt.

Matthias Darly, who has a place apart from the decorative designers of the second half of the eighteenth century, specialized both in the drawing of caricatures and of decorative detail. The majority of his productions were etched, coloured, or engraved by his own hand. Darly issued designs in the Chinese style in 1754. This was followed in 1767 with sixty vases by English, French, and Italian Masters, and the *Ornamental Architect or Young Architect's Instructor* (1770–1771), in which the Preface contains an essay on the 'Art of Design'. The date of Darly's death is not known, but he issued no caricatures after October 1780.[2] There are some signed and dated designs of Yenn, who was at work at Windsor, in the Victoria and Albert Museum, but there is on the whole a paucity of published and unpublished ornament, as compared with the output of contemporary France. Influential designers of ornament in the early nineteenth century were J. B. Papworth, who designed largely for certain manufacturers, and Charles Heathcote Tatham,[3] who brought out his etchings of ancient ornamental architecture at Rome and in Italy in 1794–1803. To him, perhaps, more than to any other person may be attributed the development of early nineteenth-century Anglo-Greek taste.[4]

Plaster Work, Scagliola and other Decorative Processes

*The Work of Robert Adam—Cast Medallions—Scagliola, Marble and Gilding—
Colour Schemes—The Etruscan Style—Marbling and Graining*

STUCCO came into use in the earlier years of the eighteenth century as being better adapted than wainscot for covering large wall surfaces of halls, saloons, and living rooms and also as conforming to the Palladian treatment of interiors. By the middle years of the century plaster decoration was in the hand of Italian craftsmen who fashioned figure subjects in relief for walls and ceilings of the great houses.

For formal treatment Robert Adam revived the Roman method of diapers of lacunæ enriched with rosettes, both in flat ceilings, and in the domes of rotundas and semi-domes of apses. An early effort in free design is seen in the modelled foliated scrolls in the cove of the Kedleston drawing-room (the sketch for which is dated 1759). With the exception of the ceiling of the hall at Syon House, which has large crossed ribs of considerable projection, Adam did not make use of wide ribs or heavy mouldings in setting out his ceilings, though in defining compartment ceilings he states that this mode is not one to which he has any objection. The setting-out is, however, emphasized in certain cases by enriched ribs, as in the breakfast-room ceiling at Harewood House, Yorkshire, and the anteroom of Syon House (Fig. 125), but the projection is slight. Massive ribbing, however, is shown in a ceiling designed by Sir William Chambers in a room at Cumberland House,[5] allied in both cases with small scale ornamental detail. A treatment (described at this period as 'mosaic') used by Robert Adam in his early work, consists of panelled octagons and lozenges. A design (dated March 1761) in the Soane Museum, which was carried out in the long gallery at Croome Court, is an early example. In Adam's matured style, plaster-work reached the delicacy of the flat and elegant Roman stucco that had impressed

[1] Plate 11. 'This ceiling is executed for the Right Hon. the Lord de Montalt by Mr. Edward Robbins.' [2] *English Furniture Designers*, p. 51. [3] 1772–1842. [4] *Architectural Publication Society's Dictionary*, sub voc. 'Furniture'. [5] Now Demolished.

126   The Long Gallery, Syon House, Isleworth, *circa 1765*, by Robert Adam. The walls are divided into units contained by four pilaster divisions, the decoration of the pilasters by Pergolesi

127 The Hall, Harewood House, Yorkshire, by Robert Adam, dated 1767. The walls divided by engaged columns of the Doric order

128 The Ballroom, Lansdowne House, London, as finished by Robert Smirke, from a design by George Dance, 1786–1819

129   The Dining-room, Crichel House, Dorset. Late eighteenth century

130   The Saloon, Boodle's Club, London, 1765. Attributed to John Crunden

131 The Drawing-room, Crichel House, Dorset. Late eighteenth century

132   The Drawing-room, Attingham House, Shropshire, *circa 1782*, by George Stuart'

133   The Hall, Dodington Park, Gloucestershire, 1798–1808, by James Wyatt. The columns of scagliola

134   The Drawing-room

135   The Upper landing

DODINGTON PARK, GLOUCESTERSHIRE, 1798–1808, BY JAMES WYATT

136 Providence House, Rhode Island, U.S.A., *circa* 1810

137 The Library, Dodington Park, Gloucestershire, 1798–1808, by James Wyatt

138   The Entrance Hall, Attingham House, Shropshire, *circa* 1782, by George Stuart

140 The Breakfast Room Ceiling, Harewood House, Yorkshire. After a design by Robert Adam, dated 1769. Plaster work by Joseph Rose

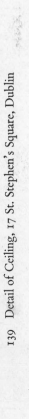

139 Detail of Ceiling, 17 St. Stephen's Square, Dublin

141 Detail of the Dining-room Ceiling

142 The Ceiling of the East Hall

CRICHEL HOUSE, DORSET. LATE EIGHTEENTH CENTURY

143   A section of the Dining-room Ceiling, Attingham, Shropshire, 1782–85. *Vide* Fig. 145

144   The Drawing-room Ceiling, Crichel House, Dorset. Late eighteenth century

146   Ceiling of the Boudoir

145   Detail of the Dining-room Ceiling

ATTINGHAM HOUSE, SHROPSHIRE, 1782, BY GEORGE STUART

148   The Stairway, Coleman-Hollister House, Greenfield,
Massachusetts, U.S.A., *circa 1807*

147   Room on the ground floor, Dodington Park, Gloucestershire,
by James Wyatt, 1798–1808

149   The Hall, Heveningham, Suffolk, *circa* 1788–99, by James Wyatt

150   The Etruscan Room, Osterley, Middlesex, *circa* 1775, by Robert Adam

151   The Print Room, Woodhall Park, Hertfordshire, *circa* 1777

152   The Gallery Ceiling, Harewood House, Yorkshire, 1769, by Robert Adam. Painted panels by Rebecca.
Plaster work by Joseph Rose

153   The Committee Room Ceiling, Bank of England, London, by Sir Robert Taylor, *circa* 1775

154   The Hall, showing screen and columns, Dodington Park, Gloucestershire, 1798–1808, by James Wyatt

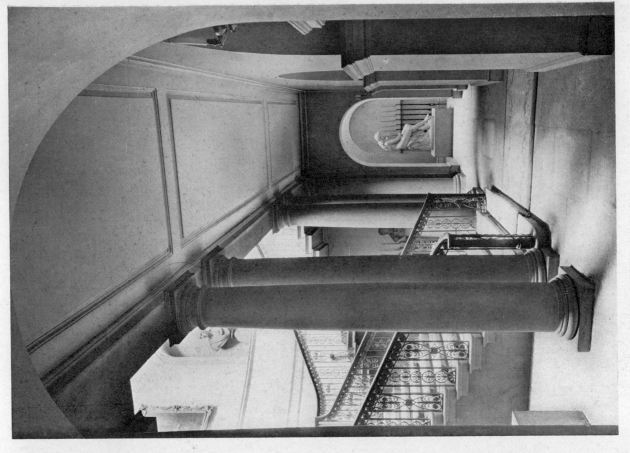

156   The Staircase Hall, Wentworth Woodhouse, Yorkshire, *circa* 1770,
by John Carr

155   The Staircase, Trinity House, Tower Hill, London, *circa* 1793–96,
by Samuel Wyatt (now destroyed)

158   The arched Screen between the Hall and Staircase, Chicheley, Buckinghamshire, an Early Georgian addition

157   The East Hall, Crichel House, Dorset. Late eighteenth century

159　The first floor Staircase Hall, Crichel House, Dorset. Late eighteenth century

160 The first floor landing, Dodington Park, Gloucestershire, 1798–1808, by James Wyatt

161   The Staircase, Harewood House, Yorkshire, 1769, by Robert Adam

162　The Entrance Hall, Dodington Park, Gloucestershire, 1798–1808, by James Wyatt

164   The Court Room, Bank of England, London, *circa 1775*,
by Sir Robert Taylor

163   Detail of the Painted Saloon, Heveningham, Suffolk, *circa 1788–99*,
by James Wyatt

167 The Small Drawing-room, Attingham, Shropshire, *circa* 1782, by George Stuart

166 Doorway into the Small Hall, Crichel House, Dorset. Late eighteenth century

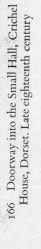

165 The Boudoir in the East Wing, Attingham, Shropshire, *circa* 1782, by George Stuart

169   The Hall, Courteenhall, Northamptonshire, 1791–93, by Samuel Saxon

168   Detail of Wall and Chimney-piece at 4 Grafton Street, London, *circa* 1770

James Adam in his studies in Italy. Square ceilings are usually treated with an ornament arranged on a concentric basis; but in oblongs a central square was often set out with narrow oblongs at either end. 'The smaller compartments', as Chambers writes, 'are generally arranged round the sides of the ceiling, leaving a large compartment round, square, or octagonal in the centre'. In rooms with apsidal terminations a radiating fan treatment is usual. In this stucco-work was often inserted a series of painted panels and medallions. In a design for the gallery ceiling at Harewood House (dated 1769), panel paintings are indicated, laced about with thin lines of flowing ornament.

Modelled or cast bas-relief medallions and panels had been employed before the reign of George III, but were much more freely used in the late eighteenth century. Examples of this treatment are the panels set within large panels in the dining-room at Shardeloes, which are the centre of a system of arabesques; a panel with a group of Greek girls with linked hands, which appears both at Penn House, Great Portland Street, and as the tablet set in the frieze above the door in the back parlour of Pitzhanger Manor (Fig. 175). A recurrent type is the single figure of a dancing nymph or musician, who appears in 4 Grafton Street, the eating-room of Pitzhanger Manor, and elsewhere.

For halls, medallions or panels of grouped Roman arms were used by Robert Adam, as in the porter's hall of 20 St. James's Square, the entrance hall at Newby, in the anteroom at Syon House, where *amorini* aid in supporting an immense gilded trophy of Roman body armour, enriched shields of various shapes, lances, helmets and quivers (Fig. 125). The interest of the collectors of the period in Greek vases is responsible for the vogue of the bas-relief vase or urn as a decorative wall panel, which appears in the overdoor panels in the entrance hall at Newby, and in the hall at Syon House.

The flow of the lines of delicate ornament in ceiling designs was attentively studied, minutely enriched narrow ribs or loopings and festoonings of husks form the setting-out, enlivened by elements from Roman ornament, gryphons, sphinxes, urns, candelabra and foliated creatures issuing from scrolls. Circles and semicircles enriched with radial flutings appear rather too frequently in some interiors of their eighteenth century. Such elements were more formally treated than in contemporary French decoration. Fresh and naturalistic *motifs* of decoration are occasionally drawn upon, as in the dining-room at Drayton,[1] and where the panel on the chimney-breast has a figure of Apollo in relief, framed in bay leaves; above is hung a group of musical instruments; the panels on either side have mirrors framed in sprays of ivy; the overdoor and mural panels are also treated with foliage and framed in reeded and ribboned mouldings, and in the cove of the ceiling are interlacing trails of vine branches, naturalistically coloured. The inception and development of this style of stucco decoration is due to Robert Adam, whose style was assimilated by the younger George Dance and Thomas Leverton. The scale of detail diminished in the late years of the century. In the domestic work of Henry Holland, the reduction of amount of ornament continues; in the dining-room at Southill, the ceiling is divided by ribs into large panels; in the ceiling of the small painted room, a foliage border is carried out in gilt metal. In the ceiling decoration for Carlton House, illustrated by Pyne, his detail is massive and Roman. A ceiling is described as formed as four deep coves, panelled and ornamented, springing from a well-proportioned enriched cornice, which supports a handsome framework divided into three panels, separated by stucco work richly gilt. The large central panel is embellished by plaster figures in relief representing the elements, also tillage, harvest, etc., and the covers with combinations of boys, griffins, and foliated ornaments.[2] Colouring either the ornament, or ground, or both, prevailed during this period of low-relief ornamentation. The usual method was to gild all the ornament, to leave the grounds white, pearl, straw-colour, light blue, 'or any other tint proper to set off the gilding and ornament to the best advantage'.[3]

The names of plaster-workers have been in a few cases recorded. Joseph Rose, who worked for Adam at Kenwood, Harewood, Syon, Newby, and Kedleston, carried out the detailed office designs

---

[1] Dating soon after 1770. [2] *Royal Residences*, vol. iii. p. 20. [3] *Works in Architecture*, 1778–1822, vol. i. Part 2, p. 10.

prepared for him. He was described by a contemporary as 'the first man in the kingdom as a plasterer'.[1] There are several sketches in colour, ink and wash in his note books marked Mr. Rose's Designs. At Sledmere, however, he appears as an independent designer of ornament and architectural adviser to Sir Christopher Sykes. He also worked for James Wyatt at the Pantheon, and Castle Coole. Roberts, an Oxford plasterer, made a name in the late eighteenth century, for Mrs. Lybbe Powys mentions at Heythrop, in 1778, 'very fine stucco ornament' by his hand. 'In the arches over the doorway', she adds, are 'Fables of Æsop, finely executed in stucco, with wreathes of vine leaves'.[2] His work is also recorded at Christ Church, Oxford and the Codrington Library, All Souls.

The original member of the firm of George Jackson of Rathbone Place, which was founded about 1780, was associated with Robert Adam, and there is a tradition that composition was introduced by him; the late Georgian boxwood moulds, carved with great precision and delicacy, remain in the firms' possession, and are still in use, together with a large and interesting collection of detail. Patroli, 'an Italian artist of great ingenuity', was employed for a long time at Claydon; and there are recognizable Italian characteristics in the delicate and florid plaster-work of the staircase hall and library.

John Papworth[3] was apprenticed to learn the trade of a plasterer and stuccoist with Rose; 'architect, plasterer, and builder', as he styled himself in 1795; and became 'almost the only man of his day in this art, having five hundred men at work under him'. He worked for Sir William Chambers, and, under the Board of Works, at Greenwich Hospital Chapel and Buckingham House; and on his death in 1799 his business was carried on by his eldest son Thomas, 'plasterer to His Majesty's Board of Works', until his death in 1814.[4] Before his death, however, the interest of plaster ornament declined; and cornice and the central ornament of a rose that lingered during the nineteenth century were formal survivals. Many of these ornaments were made, at a very low price, of *papier-mâché*.[5]

SCAGLIOLA, MARBLE AND GILDING—COLOUR SCHEMES—THE ETRUSCAN STYLE— MARBLING AND GRAINING

The employment of foreign marble was from its expense restricted, and the cartage, the brittleness of the substance, and the delay in procuring and shipping large blocks were further difficulties in the way of its use. Thus the employment of the columns of verde antique found in the bed of the Tiber for the anteroom at Syon House (Fig. 125), which gives the keynote to Robert Adam's Roman scheme of decoration for that room, is exceptional. At Kedleston, Robert Adam made use of the effective tawny-veined alabaster for the columns of the great hall, and for the window and door-cases of the drawing-room, which was brought from the neighbouring pits at Chellaston.

Among the processes introduced in England at this time was scagliola, and James Adam, in a diary kept while he was abroad, notices scagliola at Florence which could be used for various purposes; 'for instance, for columns resembling different marbles, for tables resembling mosaic work, for most elegant floors'.[6] It was compounded of gypsum, which, after being broken into small pieces and calcined, was reduced to powder or plaster of Paris; it was then passed through a sieve, and mixed with Flanders glue, isinglass, and the colouring matter of the hue required. Thus prepared it was applied to the surface to be coated, and smoothed and polished. The earliest use of scagliola in England is credited to James Wyatt in the Pantheon in Oxford Street, which was opened in January 1772. In the 1783 edition of Ralph's *Critical Observations* it is stated that the columns of the Pantheon are formed of a 'newly invented composition which rivals the finest marbles in colour and hardness'.[7] Scagliola is found in houses which the Wyatts built or decorated, such as Trinity House, Heaton Park, 15 St.

[1] *Letters of Sir Thomas Robinson*, 1768, Architectural Review, vol. lx.   [2] *Passages from the Diary of Mrs. Lybbe Powys*, 1899, p. 200.   [3] 1750–1799.
[4] *Wyatt Papworth, John B. Papworth*, 1879, p. 5.   [5] Loudon, *Cottage, Farm, and Villa Architecture*, 1833, p. 274.   [6] *Library of Fine Arts*, vol. ii.
No. 9, October 1831.   [7] *Critical Observations of the Public Buildings of London*, 1783.

James's Square and Heveningham (Fig. 149). An Italian, Domenico Bartoli, probably had the monopoly of its production, and his bills for the supply of scagliola columns are preserved at 15 St. James's Square; at Buckland a memorandum records that the columns were the work of Signor Bartoli, who also supplied Sir Rowland Winn with marble tables[1] inlaid with scagliola for Nostell, the sixteen columns imitating Sicilian jasper in the saloon at Stowe were also supplied by him. Its cheapness, lustre and durability were much admired at this period, and 'the artists succeed in an astonishing degree with the most beautiful marble, such as Sienna, jasper, brocatello, and porphyry; it is hard, and when finished bears a very fine polish, and is laid on brick in the manner of stucco and worked off with iron tools'.[2] From its plasticity before it sets it was found superior to marble for inlaying, and was used freely for ornamenting chimney-pieces, and also in cabinet work. The anteroom of Syon House has richly coloured and polished scagliola flooring in which the pattern is related to that of the ceiling (Fig. 125), the colouring composed of a yellow, a bright and dark red, and a greenish-grey and blue. The production of scagliola continued in the early nineteenth century, when vases, stands for busts, and columns serving as candelabras were manufactured, as well as columns in rooms 'of a superior description'.[3]

Gilding appears in the early houses decorated by Robert Adam. In the anteroom of Syon House, which is Roman in its imperial splendour, the capitals of the columns, the enrichments of the frieze, and the statues above the columns, and the large panels of military trophies on each side of the door leading into the entrance hall are gilt (Fig. 125). In the last years of the century, however, a reaction set in against gilding, and interiors are praised for having no tinsel or tawdriness about them. 'Little gilding'[4] is noted in Mrs. Delany's description of Luton, the house of Adam's patron, Lord Bute; and Walpole, returning from Portman House in 1782, remembers that 'there was not a morsel of gilding'; 'it is grand', he writes, 'not tawdry, nor larded and embroidered and pomponned with shreds and remnants of clinquant'.[5] A revival of gilding accompanied the French methods employed at Carlton House by Holland, and in the anteroom the walls are described as bright blue, surrounded by mouldings of burnished gold.[6] The chosen tints of the latter part of the eighteenth century were light secondary colours such as pink, pea-green, light blue, lavender, used either singly or combined, but never primary colours. Adam's coloured sketches at the Soane Museum are better evidence today of the effect he aimed at than most of his decorations, which have faded. The sketch of the drawing-room ceiling at Kedleston show a full colour scheme which still in part exists; the grounds of the cove is pink and of its medallions cream; the grounds of the central portion of the ceiling are pink and blue. In the Soane Museum drawings the ceiling of Lady Scarsdale's dressing-room has portions brilliantly coloured rose, green, and gold, and the ceiling of a projected book-room is tinted pea-green, pink and blue. To this light tonality there was one exception, the Etruscan manner. Adam sets forth his array of authorities for this mode of decoration which 'differs from anything hitherto practised in Europe', of which the ornaments and colouring were imitated from vases and urns. The first experiment in this colouring was made in Lord Derby's house in Grosvenor Square, and other Etruscan rooms were immediately designed 'for the house of Earl Bathurst, and that of the Countess Dowager of Home in town, and at Mr. Child's at Osterley Park'.[7] (Fig. 150). At Newtimber in Sussex the hall still retains its Etruscan decoration, consisting of enlarged copies of scenes from vase-paintings arranged in framed panels. At Osterley, Walpole describes the anteroom as 'painted all over like Wedgwood's ware with black and yellow small grotesques. 'I never saw such a profound tumble into bathos. It is going out of a palace into a potters' field'.[8] The famous room still remains as a complete example of the Etruscan colouring, and follows in every detail Adam's design, dated October 1775. The Etruscan Hall at Woodhall, and the small anteroom to the saloon at Heveningham date a few years later. The latter is

[1] Richler & Bartoli's bill (1777) is for 'two statuary Tables inlaid of Scagliola according to Messrs. Adam's disaing (*sic*). Brockwell, *The Nostell Collection*, 1915, p. 29. [2] Chambers's *Encyclopædia*, ed. 1783 (*sub voc.*). [3] Loudon, *Cottage, Farm, and Villa Architecture*, 1857, p. 1012. [4] In September 1774. *Life and Correspondence of Mrs. Delany* (Second Series), vol. ii. p. 35. [5] 14th Debruary 1782. [6] Pyne, *Royal Residences*, vol. iii. p. 40. [7] *Works*, vol. ii. preface. [8] *Letters*, 16th July 1778.

an attempt to reproduce the subject and colouring of 'Etruscan' vases, the figures being painted in terra-cotta, touched with black, on walls, ceilings and door panels.

Soane seemed to have preferred the occasional use of the stronger colours of the Empire period, yellows and Pompeian reds, in bands or masses. The revival of graining, marbling and painting in metallic colours at Carlton House, which was considered a novelty,[1] was attributed to Henry Holland, and according to another authority, French artists whose names are given as Labrière, Boileau, Dumont le Romain and Boulenger were brought over by Sheringham of Great Marlborough Street.[2] In Pyne's description and illustrations of Carlton House, silvered and bronzed ornaments are shown, as in the Rotunda, where the ornaments of the cornice and architraves are silvered and relieved by a ground of light lavender tint, while the ornaments of the frieze consisting of boys supporting festoons of foliage and fruit were painted in imitation of bronze.[3] Marbling also appeared in the entrance hall, where the walls were of granite green, which blended with the real marble and porphyry; and Soane's Breakfast Parlour at Pitzhanger Manor was described in 1832 as a 'Marble Room' (the walls and ceiling were then marbled). Graining, or the imitation of various figured and decorative woods, was occasionally employed on wood in the late eighteenth century, but was much more widely practised during the early nineteenth century, when it was recommended that all woodwork should if possible be 'grained in imitation of some natural wood, not with a view of having the imitation mistaken for the original, but rather to create an allusion to it and by a diversity of lines to produce a kind of variety and intricacy which affords more pleasure to the eye than a flat shade of colour'.[4] This widespread use of grained soft wood is said to have originated at the time of the French Revolution, when it was impossible to obtain supplies of valuable woods, and English oak was requisitioned for ship-building, so that little but deal and beech was to be had. Maple wood was imitated after about 1817,[5] and the careful copying of various woods by skilful veining and reproduction of knots, veins, spots, swirls and 'mottles' made graining very popular until the middle years of the nineteenth century, when it was repudiated as a sham by enthusiasts.[6]

Interior Features

The Hall and Staircase—The Chimney-piece—The Door and Door-case

THE problem of allotting space between a hall and staircase differs in town and country houses. In country houses it was not Adam's practice to sacrifice undue space to a staircase hall, and, as may be seen at Kedleston, he deviates from Paine's plan (by which a top-lighted staircase hall with a double flight of steps was placed between the great hall and a circular drawing-room) and gives this space to the saloon, providing elsewhere for two modest staircases. In some country houses of the late years of the century, the staircase hall is designed on a large scale and richly treated; at Heaton Park, for example, the stair rises in a double flight, and the most important room on the first floor is reached by a fine door in the centre of the upper level. In great London houses a hall sometimes gives access to the staircase hall, rising to the full height of the house, and lit by a skylight, usually oval or circular. The head of the staircase is coved and often treated with stucco ornament, and the main stairs are not carried beyond the first floor, the bedrooms above being served by secondary stairs.

[1] Mr Crace stated that his father 'remembered their introduction by French workmen at Carlton House' (*Papers read at the R.I.B.A. Session*, 1857–1858, London, 1858, p. 12).   [2] Wyatt Papworth, *John B. Papworth*, 1879, op. 11.   [3] *Royal Residences*, 1819, vol. iii. p. 24.   [4] Loudon, *Cottage, Farm, and Villa Architecture* (1833), p. 277.   [5] At this date George Morant of New Bond Street sent to J. B. Papworth a specimen of the imitation of maple wood.   [6] Gilbert Scott, *Remarks on Secular and Domestic Architecture*, 1857, p. 76.

In small London houses the floor levels are sometimes marked on the wall of the hall by a band of ornament. The head of the stair at 6 Bedford Square (at the second-floor level) is interesting in treatment. The ceiling consists of two semi-domes, enriched with fluting and supporting pendentives carrying a cornice; the end walls, which are semicircular, are plainly treated except for a bust on a console; but the side walls are panelled by enriched mouldings, and the lunette above them ornamented with bas-relief medallions. In a house designed by Thomas Leverton, No. 1 Bedford Square, the staircase (which is placed in the right-hand bay) has its walls relieved by shallow niches for tripods, vases, or statuary, and the soffits of the landings are enriched with large pateras and other ornamental detail. A staircase hall designed by Sir John Soane for the old War Office, Pall Mall,[1] was oval in plan, with a single flight of stairs with plain iron balustrading dividing at the first landing and rising to a gallery supported by Ionic columns.

The application of wrought iron to the staircase balustrade dates from the late seventeenth century, but the use of both wrought and cast iron was stimulated in the late eighteenth century by the preference for a circular stair, describing one sweeping curve from floor to floor, in which every part was made subservient to its upward gliding curve. Iron balustrading was considered much 'superior to wood, both for strength and beauty'; the continuous handrail of moulded mahogany was of the lightest and the balustrading was of necessity also of the lightest ironwork. The forms of these iron panels or balusters are varied; an S-shaped stanchion is found in 8 Grosvenor Square, Ely House,[2] and elsewhere, sometimes separated with vertical rods. In Adam's designs, the standard sometimes takes the form of an open baluster of pilaster or lyre-pattern, linked by festoons of husks. In a sketch for the handrail of Gawthorp (Harewood) House, in the same collection, the design, which is of two heart-shaped forms enclosing an anthemium and linked in the centre by rosettes and scrolls, is adapted to the rake of the stair.[3] A simpler form of Adam balustrading consists of close-set vertical bars, enclosing ornament of the anthemium type both at the top and bottom of the panel, as at Harewood House and Kenwood. At Trinity House the balustrade of the semicircular staircase consisted of a series of S-shaped standards, divided at intervals by a richer panel filled in with small detail (Fig. 153). At Nos. 20 and 32 Bedford Square, the balustrading is of vertical wrought-iron bars, but at the ends and middle of each flight are panels of S-scroll design; at No. 1, in the same Square, the balustrading is of pairs of vertical bars alternating with an ornamental baluster having gilt bronze enrichments. In the old War Office (now demolished) the plain curved wrought-iron bars which did duty as a balustrade witness to the growing severity and impoverishment of design. Cast iron was much used in the late eighteenth century for constructional and decorative purposes, and Robert Adam's balustrades are usually of cast iron, but minute detail such as pateras and rosettes were of brass or lead cast on to an iron centre bar, and cast-lead panels were sometimes introduced, as the example at Belvedere College, Dublin, which was completed in 1786, and at Heveningham, where cast oval medallions of classical character add interest to the delicate ironwork of the panels.

THE CHIMNEY-PIECE

In the first years of George III's reign, the massive types of the Palladian school were still continued. Chimney-pieces with figures in the round were designed by Robert Adam, as in the banqueting-room at Croome Court (1763), the drawing-room at Kedleston, and the dining-room (1777) at Harewood House. Chimney-pieces are known to have been designed by Paine, and executed under his supervision, for he kept a statuary for that purpose.[4] As the half-century advanced, a lighter treatment prevailed.

[1] Now demolished. [2] Department of Engraving, Illustration and Design, Victoria and Albert Museum. [3] Clavering, *Carpenter's* Vade *Mecum*, 1776, p. 29. [4] 'Letters of Sir W. Chambers, 1769', *Journal of the R.I.B.A.*, 1892, p. 4. Furnishing chimney-pieces 'as well and upon as each terms as any other tradesman'.

Of the 'continued' type, there are instances, such as Adam's chimney-piece in the dining-room at Syon House, of which the lower structure is of marble, the upper of stucco enclosing a bas-relief panel. The space above the simple chimney-piece was often treated as a focal point in the room by the addition of a bas-relief or a large mirror. The sculpture is notable for the minute finish. Some of the most refined designs are those in which an order is used, and in which statuary side columns, either detached or of three-quarter projection, are contrasted with coloured marble backgrounds and support an entablature enriched with sculptured detail or inlay. In another type of chimney-piece of still slighter projection, the panelled jambs and lintel receive low-relief ornament. In a few cases in the late years of the eighteenth century, the frieze is omitted, as in the dining-room chimney-piece of No. 13, and in the ground floor front room of No. 41 Bedford Square, which have Ionic columns carrying the cornice directly. There was less attempt to secure rare marbles than in the Palladian period, but, according to the *Builder's Magazine* (1774), 'Sienna was common, also the green Anglesea kind and green and white Egyptian'. In the state bedroom and music-room at Kedleston, marble is combined with a local material, Blue John spar. The material, and the skilled craftsmanship of the marble-cutters and sculptors added considerably to the expense of finishing and decoration of a house. At Fonthill,[1] Mrs. Lybbe Powys notices that the 'chimney-pieces all over the house are elegant to a degree, even those in the attics must have cost an immense sum, all of statuary or Sienna marble', and at Heythrop (which she visited in 1778), the fine statuary marble chimney-piece cost £1500.

Adam's later designs show his increasing love for colour and are tinted to show the use of coloured compositions as inlay in marble, an art long established in Italy for the decoration of table-tops and chimney-pieces. Two chimney-pieces in old Derby House, Grosvenor Square, are described by Adam as of statuary marble inlaid with coloured scagliola,[2] and a sketch in the Soane Museum[3] for the second drawing-room at Lady Home's in Portman Square (which is designed for inlay), has in addition painted the table in oval medallions. The same combination of inlay and painting appears in the white marble chimney-piece in the small sitting room on the first floor at No. 20 St. James's Square, where the tablet and blockings are enriched with classic subjects in well-preserved encaustic painting, while the frieze is inlaid with swags of green marble. The prevalent fashion for painting upon marble is noticed by Richardson in his *New Collection* (1781). Some inlaid work of this character in Dublin during the latter part of the century is attributed to a Peter Bossi, an elusive figure said to have been an inlayer in marble and stucco-worker, who guarded the secret of his method and took every precaution against his work being imitated. The number of English chimney-pieces inlaid with coloured compositions, however, seems inconsistent with a monopoly of Bossi's.[4] In less important rooms, wood was substituted, ornamented with detail in painted composition, by which an effect was obtained at much less expense than by the marble mason or wood-carver.

The application of ormolu was introduced by Robert Adam in the white statuary chimney-piece in the drawing-room at Syon House, where the Corinthian capitals, the ornament of the frieze, and the vertical panels between the architrave and the columns, the dentils, and the beading in the flutes of the columns are of ormolu, which replaces sculpture. Bronze and ormolu appliqués were also used by Holland in his decoration at Carlton House in the Throne room, where the white marble chimney-piece was supported by satyrs in bronze and ormolu, and the frieze of grey marble was enriched by ormolu ornament.[5]

Cast tin or pewter ornaments of thin plate stamped in relief as a substitute for carving were introduced by Matthew Boulton, who at one time took up the trade of enriching chimney-pieces, and, unlike Wedgwood, won the patronage of the builders.[6] These applied ornaments when painted had the appearance of carving. Sometimes the entire extent of the frieze was sculptured, as in the front

[1] *Passages from the Diaries of Mrs Lybbe Powys*, p. 167.　　[2] *Works in Architecture*, vol. ii. No. 1, p. 3.　　[3] Dated 1st February 1775.　　[4] According to *The Georgian Society* he worked in Dublin from 1785 (or a little earlier) down to 1798, in which year owing to being implicated in the revolutionary movement, he deemed it advisable to leave Dublin. *Georgian Society*, vol. i. p. 22.　　[5] *Royal Residences*, vol. iii. p. 26　　[6] Meteyard's *Life of Wedgwood*, vol. ii. p. 372.

room on the first floor of No. 20, and the Board Room of No. 15 St. James's Square. The frieze often centred in a tablet, a central panel whose design was carefully considered; in a number of Georgian dining-rooms the tablet is carved with a sacrifice to Bacchus; and the rape of Europa, the Choice of Hercules, 'Roman marriages', Apollo and the Muses never seem to have lost their hold upon the dilettanti.

The demand for tablets and friezes for the finer chimney-pieces attracted both native and foreign sculptors. Joseph Wilton (1722–1803) carved chimney-pieces for houses built by Sir William Chambers; and John Bacon (1735–1805), 'the most prolific and most fortunate sculptor of the day' is responsible for a marble chimney-piece in the Green Presence Chamber in Windsor Castle. The Italian Locatelli[1] who worked for Adam, executed a marble chimney-piece at Harewood House.

Among the generation of sculptors born after the middle of the eighteenth century, two names only need be recorded, Thomas Proctor,[2] and John Deare. John Deare,[3] who was apprenticed to the marble mason, Carter of Piccadilly, in 1775, was employed at the early age of sixteen in carving chimney-pieces. 'He modelled bas-reliefs of the Seasons; each consisting of eight naked boys variously employed, according to the Season they were intended to represent, being intended as tablets for chimney-pieces, and executed with the greatest rapidity'.

The taste for carved and modelled bas-reliefs as architectural accessories suggested to Josiah Wedgwood[4] that his moulded ware in plaques and panels might well take their place. Flaxman was designing bas-reliefs for chimney-pieces for the firm in 1776, and in 1778 he has a 'glorious assortment' including the marriage of Cupid and Psyche, Homer with a frieze of Apollo and the Muses, and a sacrifice to Flora; but the innovation was not welcomed either by the architects or the public. 'I know they are much cheaper at that price', Wedgwood writes, 'than marble, and every way better, but people will not compare things which they conceive to be made out of moulds, or perhaps stamped at a blow like the Birmingham articles, with carving in natural stones where they are certain no moulding, casting, or stamping can be done'.[5] Sir William Chambers and Wyatt were constant to their prejudices; Wedgwood, however, was able to convert Capability Brown, who 'preferred them greatly to sculpture in marble'. A complete chimney-piece of Wedgwood's ware, composed of several pieces, is illustrated in Meteyard's *Life of Wedgwood*.[6] These sets generally consisted of five or seven pieces, the central feature being a tablet of considerable length; and on either side of this were smaller plaques. A number of such chimney-piece sets in blue and white jasper were included in the sale of the stock in the warehouse in 1781.

THE DOOR AND DOOR-CASE

Doors of communication continued to be placed as far as possible in a line; but the excessive use of feigned in addition to actual doors (which had been a characteristic of the Palladian treatment) was given up; as it was recognized that in the English climate the fewer real doors a room has, the more it will be comfortably habitable,[7] and that the feigned door occupied space which might be given to decoration. The door-case is rarely treated with an order[8] by Robert Adam and his followers, and the pediment is discarded, but in Adam's early work, consoles support the cornice above the door. In the late eighteenth century the general treatment shows a marked flatness; usually the architrave is surmounted by an entablature with frieze and moulded cornice of slight projection; and sometimes a centre tablet with bas-relief or painted decoration is inserted, breaking into the lower members of the cornice. In the late years of the eighteenth and early nineteenth century, a reeded architrave with rosettes or pateras at the angles became the usual treatment.

[1] A chimney-piece at Harewood House was carved by Locatelli. [2] 1755–1826. [3] 1759–1795. [4] Meteyard, *Life of Josiah Wedgwood*, 1865, vol. ii. p. 364. [5] *Letter* 6th October 1778. [6] Vol. ii. p. 373. [7] *The Decorative Part of Civil Architecture*, ed. Papworth, 1826, p. 130. [8] There are examples of this treatment, however, in the library and in the drawing-room, Kedleston.

The door itself, whether of solid mahogany or painted deal, was usually six panelled, and the best form of the panels was, according to the *Builder's Magazine*, the plainest, 'that is, a long square, the two or four larger should be long upwards and the other crosswise'.[1] The panels were surrounded by a wide margin usually enriched with fluting between two shallow mouldings and having rosettes at the angles. In doorways with painted decoration these enriched mouldings are dispensed with, and the panels painted with light ornament, medallions, or flying figures.

In the increasing flatness of decoration in the last years of the eighteenth and early nineteenth century, panel mouldings were dispensed with, broad bands of ebony inlay taking their place.

[1] *Builder's Magazine*, 1774, p. 203.

170 Chinese Wall-paper of floral and bird type at Temple Newsam, Yorkshire. Hung about 1806. Reduction 1–30

V

THE REGENCY PERIOD AND REVIVED GOTHIC
(1790-1830)

Introduction: The Interior

The Work of Henry Holland and Sir John Soane—The Revived Gothic—The Chinese Taste—
Decoration in America

THE conditions of the last years of the eighteenth and early nineteenth century hemmed England in in a peculiar solitude. When Lord Holland travelled in Spain during the Peninsular War, he was looked upon with suspicion and resentment by his contemporaries. Lord Dudley writes that Lord Holland ought to be 'extremely cautious not to give rise to a suspicion of his being too much attached to foreign notions or foreign manners, which, if it once existed, would ruin him irretrievably as a public man. It is just the thing about which the inhabitants of this island are most jealous'.[1]

The years of war and high taxation fell heavily upon the labourer, but the landed aristocracy prospered. Though the pressure of certain war taxes was heavy, landlords' rents had in some cases increased fivefold between 1790 and 1812. The late years of the century were not empty of buildings, and some splendid mansions rose during the continental war. French influence was dominant in the work of Henry Holland, the friend of Fox and the Whig party, who altered and enlarged Carlton House for the Prince Regent, and 'improved' Woburn Abbey for the Duke of Bedford, built Southill in Bedfordshire for Mr. Samuel Whitbread,[2] recased and redecorated Althorp for Lord Spencer.[3] His interior decoration has a refined simplicity due to the greater concentration of ornament and his skilful manipulation of Louis XVI *motifs*. (Figs. 171, 173, 182).

During the first quarter of the nineteenth century there was a general lively interest among the educated public in pure Greek architecture. In consequence ornament was restricted, and the English interior during this period expresses a rigid discipline.

Sir John Soane, a pupil of the younger George Dance, whose early allegiance was given to Robert Adam rather than to Sir William Chambers, bridges the transitional period; he began to practise in 1780, and substituted for Adam decoration a flat and linear surface treatment (Fig. 181). In the existing examples of Soane's decoration, such as Pitzhanger Manor (Fig. 176) and his own house (now the Soane Museum) in Lincoln's Inn Fields, the detail is rigidly classic, spaced and arranged in his individual manner. A feature of decoration under Soane and during the early years of the nineteenth century, which is also characteristic of the Empire style in France, is the complete exclusion of external semi-constructional forms such as columns and entablatures as decorative adjuncts. 'It is impossible', he told his pupils, 'for me to impress too much upon your minds that modillions, mutules, dentils, and tryglyphs cannot be admitted in the interior of any edifice with even a shadow of propriety'. Instead, he made use of fretted pilasters of his own design, with capitals crowned with mouldings, and sometimes enriched with grooves or frets.

The latest classic manner was impressed upon the public by Thomas Hope, a personal friend of the

---

[1] *Letters to Ivy*, p. 58.　[2] In 1795.　[3] 1786–1789.

H

French architect Percier, who, with his collaborator Fontaine, had given a definite form to the French Empire. Thomas Hope's education was unusually prolonged. After spending eight years in studying and sketching architectural remains in Egypt, Greece, Sicily, Turkey, Syria, Spain and other countries, he settled in England in 1796, when Holland was under French occupation. The scope and scale of his wander years divided him sharply from Italian-trained architects. He seems by personal predilection to have sympathized with the rigidity of the Empire style. 'I scarcely was able to hold a pencil', he tells us, 'when instead of flowers, landscapes, and all other familiar objects, I already began dealing in those straight lines which seem so little attractive to the greatest number'. In his *Household Furniture and Decoration* (which was issued in 1807) he made most of the drawings; and the work had an immediate effect. Hope does not appear to have pushed his principles except by the publication of *Household Furniture*. Interest was concentrated upon furniture and hangings, and the walls treated as backgrounds to the furniture. Hope's style is closely derived from French originals and inspired by archaeological fantasy. 'In that style the architects of Naploeon built the monument and wrote the epitaph of Renaissance art'.[1] It is, in France as in England, a style of structural simplicity and ideal severity in ornament. In the close study of classic detail, the last resources of classic architecture seemed at length to be exhausted; and the Empire style did, in point of fact, mark the dissolution of Renaissance architecture.

Classic Room showing walls draped with curtains over panels of looking glass. From Hope 'Household Furniture and Interior Decoration,' 1807 (Plate VII).

During the late Georgian period, chimney-pieces became smaller and lighter, and are usually of the one-storeyed or 'simple' type. In Papworth's note in his edition of the *Decorative Part of Civil Architecture*, it is said that they are 'now treated rather as pieces of furniture than as integral portions of the edifice, which character they formerly maintained; immense looking-glasses with gilt frames have superseded the carved and painted superstructure of the fireplace'. Chimney-pieces in the early nineteenth century, low in proportion, and consisting of marble slabs forming jambs and lintel and a narrow shelf with rounded ends, dispense with the sculptor. The lintel and jambs were usually reeded, with a patera on the blockings. The economical boxed chimney-piece consisting of slips of marble, placed on end to form hollow pilasters, was prevalent in the early nineteenth century, this large and plain surface being rarely ornamented except by consoles to the pilasters. In 1815 Bossi complained that architects had made a change in their designs leaving out ornaments and making them so plain that they could be executed for a few pounds.

It is a 'fundamental point in Regency design that it is a style profoundly miscellaneous'.[2] There

---

[1] G. Scott, *The Architecture of Humanism* (1914), p. 49.   [2] D. Pilcher, *The Regency Style*, p. 67.

172   The Painted Parlour, Southill, Bedfordshire, 1795–1800, by Henry Holland

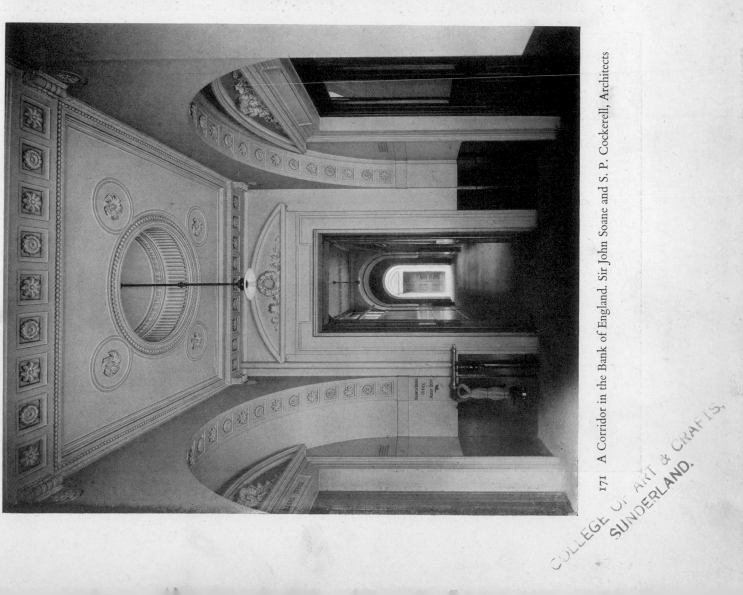

171   A Corridor in the Bank of England. Sir John Soane and S. P. Cockerell, Architects

173   The Dining-room, Southill, Bedfordshire, by Henry Holland, *circa* 1800. Decorated with painted panels. (*Vide* Fig. 182)

174   The Drawing-room, Crawley House, Bedfordshire, 1806, showing wall-paper in the Egyptian taste

175 The Assembly Room, the Stamford Hotel, Stamford, Lincolnshire. Early nineteenth century

176 The Back Parlour, Pitzhanger Manor, Ealing, *circa* 1802, by Sir John Soane

177   The Library, Barnsley Park, Gloucestershire, *circa* 1810

178   The Staircase, Pelzer House, U.S.A. Early nineteenth century

180   The Entrance Hall, The Stamford Hotel, Stamford, Lincolnshire.
Early nineteenth century

179   The First Floor Gallery, The Bedford Hotel, Brighton.
Early nineteenth century

181   The Library, Wimpole Hall, Cambridgeshire, 1790-95, by Sir John Soane

183　Detail of the Library, Barnsley Park, Gloucestershire.
Early nineteenth century

182　Detail in the Dining-room, Southill, Bedfordshire, *circa* 1800, by Henry Holland,
showing painted decoration in grisaille

was a new revival of the Chinese taste in the Brighton Pavilion (Figs. 183–185), and a revival of Gothic which extends from the early years of George II's reign to the Victorian age. The Gothic revival owed a debt to the 'relative beauty' of associated ideas; Gothic forms were 'a romantic material, rich with the charms of history'.[1] There are signs of interest in the third edition of Neve's *Complete Builders' Guide* (1736) where the modern Gothic is praised for its delicacy and whimsicality, and William Kent's addition to Rousham dates from between 1738 and 1741 (Fig. 105). The style, it was suggested, was 'congenial to our Gothic constitutions'.[2] In the middle years of the century, Richard Bentley, Horace Walpole, and Sanderson Miller attempted to revive Gothic domestic architecture and construct an interior decoration in harmony with a Gothicized exterior. A famous instance of the style is Strawberry Hill (Figs. 190, 191), which according to its owner's *Description* (1784) was designed to exhibit 'specimens of Gothic architecture as collected from standards in cathedrals and chapel tombs',[3] and 'to show how they may be applied to chimney-pieces, ceilings, windows, balustrades, etc'. But the interior was not only a cento of medieval originals; the frieze of the Round drawing room was designed by Robert Adam, the staircase balustrade by Richard Bentley (Fig. 194). His rooms were 'more the work of fancy than imitation'.[4]

Use was made of *papier mâché*, and the carved and fretted ceiling of the Holbein chamber, divided into 'star and quatrefoil' compartments, all in *papier mâché*, was a cheaper substitute for Gothic carved detail.

James Wyatt, who created a new phase of the Revival, was the most ill-fated of the group of architects designing in the 'Gothic' during the late years of the eighteenth and early nineteenth century. His first work was the decking at the old house at Lee in Kent, for which he made some plans, some Gothic and some classical. The library was admired by Horace Walpole, who considered it as having the air of 'an abbot's library, supposing it could have been exquisitely finished three hundred years ago'.[5]

Fonthill Abbey (begun in 1795 and more or less completed in 1807) was intended to have a spectacular scenic effect in both the exterior and interior. The hall was one hundred and twenty feet high, the vista of the gallery (extending through the octagon) extended for three hundred feet.

In Wyatt's Ashridge (on which he worked from 1806 until his death) there is an element of castellated work, and it would, at a later stage in the revival, have been described as Tudor. The great height given to the hall is characteristic of Wyatt's designs. No attempt was made to Gothicize the interior, except in the hall. The staircase, with its balustrade of cast iron, winds round the hall, giving it a 'most unrealistic effect in view of its supposed Gothic character'[6] (Fig. 193).

The tracery of windows, and the ornamental detail of Gothic interiors were designed to have the appearance of stonework, but were carried out in composition or cast in iron. Tracery was carried out in cast iron in the tall aspiring windows of Porden's Eaton Hall (Figs. 188, 195).

While the Gothic was in fashion, some buildings were given a range of painted windows, and medieval trimmings to put them into the mode. At Arbury, some rooms were Gothicized (Fig. 190); the ceiling of the dining-room was fan-vaulted, sides of the room broken by a canopied niche.[7]

In the library at Milton in Berkshire (Fig. 191) built-in bookcases are ranged at intervals and both bookcases and windows are given crocketed ogee heads. The chimney-piece is flanked by clustered columns.

A further revival dates from the Regency period, where Kendall, Cottingham, Blore and Rickman wrote of Gothic 'principles' and six Gothic styles were differentiated by Loudon. The 'Cathedral Gothic' of William Porden's Eaton Hall[8] which dates between 1804 and 1812, shows a consistent

[1] Geoffrey Scott, *The Architecture of Humanism*, p. 45.   [2] *The World*, 22nd March 1753.   [3] In the gallery, the great door was taken from the North door of St. Albans, the ceiling from one of the south aisles of Henry VII's chapel, the side recesses from the tomb of Archbishop Bouchier at Canterbury.   [4] Letter of Horace Walpole to Miss Berry, October 1794.   [5] Letter to Miss Berry, 17th October 1794.   [6] Dale, *James Wyatt*, 1936, p. 83.   [7] These niches have, however, casts from classic sculptures.   [8] Eaton Hall was entirely rebuilt by Alfred Waterhouse, 1870.

elaboration of the style; it was called 'a palace of celebrated if somewhat too florid magnificence'. (Figs. 188, 189, 195).

In America after the Revolution, the reliance upon English originals was continued, but the architects and builders followed newer sources, such as the *Works in Architecture of Robert and James Adam*, and Paine's *British Palladio*, the most popular of architectural handbooks. No fewer than four of Paine's works were republished in America before 1804.[1] During the early nineteenth century, there is a tendency to simplify the decoration of the wall-surface and to emphasize individual members, such as doorways, windows and chimney-pieces. The effect of interiors of this period is of a 'clear, airy and delicate dignity'. This simplification is noticeable in the treatment of the staircase balustrade, where the balustrades often take the form of plain rods, square or round (Fig. 178).

Interest in Chinese art which was revived just before the middle of the eighteenth century, was again revived during the Regency. This last revival owes something to the taste of George, Prince of Wales, whose Chinese drawing-room at Carlton House is illustrated in Sheraton's *Cabinet-maker's and Upholsterers' Drawing Book*. In this room, the walls were divided by 'Chinese columns' and the panels painted with 'Chinese views and little scenes'. The Regent's taste was also shown in the decoration of the Brighton Pavilion, which took its final form between 1815 and 1822 (Figs. 185, 187).

Wall-Hangings

Textiles—Paper Hangings—Chinese Papers

BOTH tapestries and the less durable silks and velvets were used for wall coverings. The greater number of tapestries in English houses are of continental make, principally imported from Brussels. Occasionally these were ordered of the exact size to fill the wall spaces, but more frequently they seem to have been purchased in sets of three or five, and consequently are often carried round the corners of the room. In the stock of tapestries kept at Brussels, spaces in the middle of the top border were usually left for the coat of arms or cipher of the purchaser. In the letter which the Duke of Marlborough wrote in July 1708[2]: 'I send my coat of arms as they are to be put on the hangings now making at Brussels, so that I desire you will send for Vanbrugh, so that he should take care that the crown and arms on the hangings already come over be exactly as this is'. In the late seventeenth and early eighteenth centuries, Brussels, or its rival the Gobelins, were in fashion. A number of tapestry hangings survive; but silks and velvets have nearly all perished; and we can only judge of their effect where a wise conservatism has replaced the original work with an accurate reproduction, as at Ham House.[3] The inventory of the contents of that house in 1679 show that a combination of colours was aimed at. The blue drawing-room was hung with panelled stuff, another room hung with mohair bordered with clouded satin. The bedchamber 'within the best drawing-room' was hung with panels of yellow damask, each panel fringed and framed with blue mohair.

The dating of damasks and velvets at Hampton Court Palace can be checked by the estimates and accounts in the Public Record Office. A yellow and crimson damask that once hung on the walls of a closet at the palace was supplied in 1701, and was woven with the William III motto *Je main tiend dray* and military trophies. Pieces of this material survive covering some stools in the Private drawing-room.

During the eighteenth century damasks and large patterned velvets of Italian manufacture were hung on the walls. When Sarah, Duchess of Marlborough was furnishing Blenheim, and the Earl of

---

[1] Fiske Kimball, *American Domestic Architecture*, p. 150.   [2] Quoted by E. Colville in *Duchess Sarah* (1904).   [3] *e.g.* the miniature room, where the damask hangings reproduce the original damask.

184 Wall-paper of Chinese type, of English manufacture. About 1770. Outline
printed from an engraved block, and the colours hand-painted

185 The Banqueting Room, Brighton Pavilion, 1817. The walls painted with Chinese scenes. The ceiling represents an Eastern sky, partly hidden by a plantain

186 The Corridor, formerly the Chinese gallery, Brighton Pavilion, 1819–22. The walls painted with bamboos and flowering shrubs in the Chinese taste

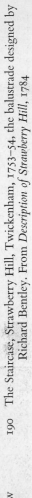

190 The Staircase, Strawberry Hill, Twickenham, 1753–54, the balustrade designed by Richard Bentley. From *Description of Strawberry Hill*, 1784

189 The Staircase, Eaton Hall, Cheshire, *circa* 1804–12, by William Porden (now replaced). From Buckler's *Views of Eaton Hall*, 1826

191   Milton House, near Didcot, Berkshire. The Gothic Library, *circa* 1760

192   The Library, Arbury Hall, Warwickshire, 1789, showing Gothic treatment of the chimney-pieces and walls

193   The Staircase in the Entrance Hall, Ashridge House, Hertfordshire, by James Wyatt. Between 1806 and 1813

194 The Library, Strawberry Hill, Twickenham, *circa* 1761. From *Description of Strawberry Hill*, 1784

195 The Library, Eaton Hall, Cheshire, 1804–12, by William Porden (now replaced). From Buckler's *Views of Eaton Hall*, 1826

Manchester[1] advised her[2] that 'It is better to have rather more than less than you shall want, for in the measuring of the rooms they may be mistaken. Besides, there must be chairs, window curtains, and for doors according to the manner of Italy, which looks very handsome. . . . . The height of the hangings for the rooms I must know else there will be a great loss when they come to be cut to make the figures join right, for they can be made to what height you please'. Velvets in Italy were either plain, 'or the ground of one colour and the flowers of several'. Lord Rivers, in ordering some yellow damask from Italy in 1717, took the trouble to 'send the pattern from England drawn upon paper'. The Duchess of Marlborough preferred silks of one colour, and therefore refused[3] the coloured velvets the Earl of Manchester had offered her, and which had been destined for his own house at Kimbolton. Houghton and Holkham are rich in velvets and damasks. In the description of Houghton the drawing room was hung with caffoy, the saloon with crimson velvet,[4] the bedchambers with velvet, tapestry, or needle-work hangings. A letter from Sir Thomas Robinson (1741) records that Genoa velvets and damasks were so plentiful that 'this one article is the price of a good house, for in one drawing room they are to the value of £3,000'.[5] At Eastbury the 'best drawing-room was hung with flowered uncut velvet of Genoa, the dressing-room with green satin'. One bedroom was 'furnished with crimson velvet'.[6]

Though Italian velvets and damasks still held the first place, the English silk industry had become of importance by the late seventeenth century. A stimulus was given by the influx of French refugees both shortly before and after the Revocation of the Edict of Nantes, so that in 1689, 40,000 families were said to be living by silk. English velvet followed Italian models, and examples of the English type are still preserved upon the furniture at Ham House and Hampton Court. During the latter half of the eighteenth century velvets were completely displaced by silk hangings and wall-papers.

Paper did not compete with other wall hangings until the development of flock (or *tortisse*), in which flocks were scattered over a surface upon which a design had been drawn or stencilled in adhesive. After the adhesive had dried, the flocks were removed from the unpainted surface by brushing. The earliest English flock paper, which formerly hung in the Manor House, Saltfleet, above a dado, appears to date from the reign of Charles II. The paper, decorated in pink flock upon a cream ground, was hung in small oblong pieces, which were nailed to the wall with small tacks. As early as 1699, however, mention is made by Houghton of 'sheets pasted together to be as long as the height of a room'.[7] The type of design suitable for flock papers is borrowed from that of Italian velvets; and there is a remarkable series of flock papers on the walls of certain state rooms at Christchurch and Withepole House, Ipswich, dating from the sale of the house in 1732. The papers in the state bed-rooms have formal patterns in dark red flock on a white and ivory ground. One design of great beauty, borrowed directly from Italian velvet, corresponds to a paper removed from the offices of the Privy Council. These papers date from the finest period of flock papers, from about 1720 to 1750; and their merits were recognized in France, where manufacturers claimed that their goods were equal to English flock papers.[8]

Printing in distemper by means of a succession of wood blocks was developed in England in the middle of the eighteenth century, and the new papers were welcomed as an alternative to flock papers.

CHINESE PAPERS

The most interesting survivals of paperhangings are the imported hand-painted papers from China, which are considered to be cheaper reproductions of painted silk hangings made for export to

[1] Charles, fourth Earl and afterwards first Duke of Manchester.   [2] 6th July 1708. *MSS. of the Duke of Manchester at Kimbolton. Hist. Monuments Comm.*   [3] 5th August 1708.   [4] *Plans, Elevations and Sections of Houghton* (1760), p. 34.   [5] Letter to Lord Carlisle, 9th December 1731. *Hist. Monuments Comm.* (15 Report, Appendix Part VI, pp. 85–86).   [6] Cumberland (R) *Memoirs* (1807), vol. i. p. 187.   [7] *A collection for the Improvement of Trade and Industry*, 30th June 1699.   [8] In 1753, Aubert, graveur en bois a Paris, announces that he makes 'papiers valontes aussi beaux et aussi parfaits que ceux d'Angleterre'. Havard, *Dictionnaire d'Ameublement*, S.V. *papiers*.

Europe. The largest and most important group is that in which the decoration consists entirely of flowers and shrubs, enlivened with birds and butterflies (Fig. 170). In some papers bird-cages are suspended from the branches of trees or shrubs. The general effect of such papers is described by a writer in 1882 as patterned 'with such vast branches and Birds of Paradise in harsh colours as people then loved to bear about on their backs and heads.'[1]

In the second group of papers the design consists of illustrations of Chinese life and industries, which appear to be later in date than the flower and shrub designs. There are frequent references to Chinese papers in English *letters* and travels of the eighteenth century. A parlour at Wanstead is described in 1722 as lined with Chinese paper, 'the figures of men, women, birds and flowers the liveliest (the author) ever saw come from that country'.[2] In the panel (Fig. 170) scenes from Chinese life are shown, including a dramatic performance watched by a crowd of spectators. Other panels from this series show lantern processions, stalls for the sale of fruit and porcelain, and a performance of acrobats. The room at Temple Newsam House (Fig. 171) was hung about 1806 with a paper of bird and flowering shrub type in delicate colours.

The excellent condition of many of these papers is partly owing to the fact that the old method of applying wall-papers is quite different from the present one. Today wall-papers are pasted on to plastered walls, the plaster walls crack and, worse still, damp comes through, thus irretrievably ruining the paper. The old method was to fasten a wooden framework over the surface of the bare walls; this was fixed to wooden wedges driven into the brick or stone work, thus leaving an air space between. On these frames were stretched canvas, and on to this canvas the wall-papers were fixed. It is for this reason that in many cases it has been possible to remove them. During the early eighteenth century, wall-papers were often varnished, which greatly increased their durability, and a lining of thick rice-paper has been found in certain examples. Sets of eighteenth-century Chinese wall-papers have been discovered in attics and lumber rooms, which have never been fixed on to walls, but are still in the neat boxes of Chinese manufacture in which they were sent to this country. (These boxes generally contain twelve lengths).

Imported Chinese paper-hangings were an expensive luxury; and there are references in the eighteenth century to the efforts of English firms to make goods as 'perfect' as the oriental (Fig. 184). In an advertisement in the *London Evening Post*, Anglo-Chinese paper-hangings are described as being 'not distinguishable from rich India paper' and 'beautifully coloured in pencil work and gilt'.[3] An account of their production is given in Dossie's *Hand Maid of the Arts*, where it is stated that the 'outlines' were formed by printing.[4] Like the imported Chinese papers, the designs can be classed in two main groups, those depicting bird and plant forms and those illustrating Chinese life and industries. So closely did these 'mock India papers' follow their Chinese models that the hanging formerly at Wotton-under-Edge,[5] of which the basis of the design is a row of trees, laden with blossoms and fruit, planted by the side of water, was formerly considered Chinese. On the back of the paper is the stamp (G.R.) ordered to be impressed on papers by an act of George I.

[1] Mrs Haweis, *Beautiful Houses*, (1882), p. 81.   [2] Macky (J.) *Journey through England* (1722), 4th edition 1724, vol. i. p. 21.   [3] 8th January 1754   [4] Ed. 1764, p. 455.   [5] Now in the Victoria and Albert Museum.

INDEX

(The numerals in heavy type refer to the *figure numbers* of the illustrations)

ABBOTT, John, 23
Acanthus ornament, 36, 38, 41
Adam, James, 59, 60, 64, 66, 76
Adam, Robert, 57-71, 75, 76; **125-127, 140,
    150, 152, 161**
Albyns, Essex, 13, 22, 23, 26; **10**
Alcoves, *see* Recesses
Aldermaston, 25; **16**
Allegorical figures, 22
Alnwick Castle, 29
Althorp, 73
America
    Chimney pieces; **73, 74, 99, 101, 104**
    Chinese influence, 48
    Colonial style, 49
    Doorways; **81, 101**
    Influence of Paine and Adam, 76
    Niches and alcoves, 49; **73, 100, 102,
        104**
    Paper hangings, 49
    Pilasters; **55, 100, 102**
    Staircases, 54; **71, 80, 103, 109-111, 113
        148, 178**
    Wainscot; **55, 99**
    Wall-painting; **55**
Amiconi, 34, 50
*Ancient Woodwork and Iron Work in
    Cambridge*, 20
Antiquities of Athens, 58
Apethorpe, 3, 22
Apocryphal wall-paintings, 11; **21-23**
Arabesque ornament, 62, 63
Arbury Hall, 75; **192**
Armorial bearings, 1, 2
Arno's Grove, Southgate, 34
Artari, Albert, 51
Arundel Collection, 57
Arundel, Earl of, 3, 4, 31
Arundel House, 4
Asgill House, Richmond, 51
Ashburnham House, 41
Ashridge House, Herts., 75; **193**
Aston Bury, 25
Aston Hall, 3, 22
Attingham House, Shropshire; **132, 138,
    165, 167,**
    Ceilings; **143, 145, 146**
Audley End, 2, 7, 8 22, 24-26, 62
d'Aviler, 43

BACHEGRAIG, Denbighshire, 6
Bacon, John, 71
Bacon's House, Gorhambury, 25
Badminton, Glos., 15; **3, 50**

Bagutti, *plasterer*, 51
Baker, *wall-painter*, 11
Balcarres House, Scotland, 23
Balusters, *see* Staircases
Banbury, Reindeer Inn, 17, 22
Bank of England, 59; **153, 164, 171**
Barbet, 9, 31, 42
Barnsley Park, Glos.; **177, 183**
Barnstaple, *frieze*, 23
Barrett, *painter*, 63
Bartoli, Domenico, 66, 67
Bartolozzi, 63
Bateman's, 47
Bath, 15, Queen's Square, 51; **108**
Battersea, Virginia, *staircase*; **111**
Beckingham Hall, 17-19
Beckington Abbey, 22
Bedford Square, London, 60, 61, 69, 70
Bellin, Nicholas, 5
Belton House, Lincs., 39, 60; **49**
Belucci, 34
Belvedere College, Dublin, 69
Belvedere, 51
Benjamin Hall Junior House, U.S.A.; **110**
Bentley, Richard, 75; **190**
Berkeley Square, No. 44, London, 46
Besford, *wall-paper*, 13
Bideford, *frieze*, 23
Blenheim Palace, 32-35, 47, 53, 76, 77; **1**
Blickling, 2, 23
Bluet, Sir Roger, 21
Bluom, 7
Bodington, Earl of, 45
Bohemia, Maryland, U.S.A.; **113**
Boileau, *artist*, 32 (*footnote*), 68
Bolsover, 3, 25
Bonomi, 61
Boodle's Club, London; **130**
Boringdon, Devon, 26
Bossi, Peter, 70, 74
Boston House, Brentford, 3, 8, 9, 22, 23,
    26; **29**
Boughton, 26, 32, 34; **112**
Boughton Malberbe, 12, 15, 17, 24, 28
Boulenger, *artist*, 68
Boulton, Matthew, 70
Bowen House, Havering, 35
Bradbury, *plasterer*, 37; **41, 59, 64, 75**
Bradfield, 27
Bradninch Manor, 15, 20, 26 (*footnote*),
    27
Bramshill, 7, 13, 17, 27
Brandenburgh House, Hammersmith, 47
Brandon, U.S.A.; **99**
Brettingham, Matthew, 57
Brickwall, Sussex, 36; **60**

Brighton
    Bedford Hotel; **179**
    Pavilion, 75, 76; **185-187**
Brocket Hall, 62
Bromley-by-Bow Palace, 16-18, 23
Brooke House, Hackney, 18
Broughton Castle, Oxon., 23, 27
Brown, 'Capability', 71
Brunetti, Gaetano, 49
de Bruyn, Abraham, 8, 9, 26; **29**
de Bruyn, Nicolas, 23
de Bry, Theodore, 19
Buckingham House, 66
Buckland, 61, 67
Buckland, William; **100**
Bulstrode, 34
Burghley, 1, 39
Burleigh, 34
Burley-on-the-Hill, 33, 34
Burlington House, 34, 61
Burlington, Lord, 4, 45, 50
Burton Agnes, 3, 22, 25, 26, 38 (*footnote*)
Bury Hall, Edmonton, 23

CAMBRIDGE
    Christ's College, 13
    Inlay work at, 20
    King's College Chapel, 5
    Queen's College, 6, 14
    St. John's College, 22
    Trinity College, 19, 30, 39
Campbell, Colin, 46, 47
Campions, Saffron Walden, 10
Canaletto, 34, 63
Canonbury, 51
Canons, 51
Canons Ashby, 22, 26, 43
Carbrook Hall, 15
Carlton House, 65, 67, 68, 70, 73, 76
Carpenters' Company Hall, 11
Carr, John; **156**
Carter, *chimney-piece maker*, 55, 71
Carter, Francis, 30 (*footnote*)
Carter's Grove, U.S.A., 49; **109**
Carving (and *see* Chimney-pieces, Screens,
    Wainscot, etc.)
    Early Renaissance, 18-20
    Late Stuart, 38-40
        Architectural orders, 8, 9
        Caryatids, 8, 19, 20
        Dutch influence, 7, 32
        Flemish influence, 6-8, 19
        Grotesque ornament, 8,9 (*diagram*), 19
        Italian influence, 18
        Military trophies, 39

Carving—*continued*
    Oak carvings, 38
    Pear wood, 39
    Picture frames, 39, 40; **77**
    'Romayne' work, 18
    Stone and marble effects, 19
    Strapwork, 8, 19, 20
    Swags, 38, 39
    Trophies; **77**
Caryatids, 8, 19, 20, 26
Casali, Andrea, 50
Cassel, Richard; **107**
Cassiobury, 34, 39
Castle Ashby, 23; **17, 18**
Castle Coole, 66
Castle Howard, 32, 34, 43; **43**
Caux, Solomon and Isaac, 9, 31
Caylus, Comte de, 58
Cedar panelling, 38; **38**
Ceilings
    Early Renaissance, 12, 21–24; **2, 4, 13**
        Painted and gilded, 12
        Central panels, 22; **15**
        Pendants, 24; **2**
    Late Stuart, 33–37; **32, 34, 40, 41, 45, 53, 59, 64, 75**
        Painted, 33–36; **34, 40, 41**
    Early Georgian, 50–52; **85, 89, 90, 96–98**
        Painted, 50, 51
        Rococo ornament, 51, 52; **90**
        Singeries, 51; **33**
    Classical Revival, 59, 64–66; **139, 140, 141–146, 152, 153**
        Designs by Adam, 59, 60, 64, 65; **140, 152**
        Painted compartments, 61, 65; **142–144, 152**
    Regency and Revived Gothic, 75; **194, 195**
Chambers, Sir William, 48, 55, 59–62, 64, 65, 71
Chandeliers, 46
Chandos House, 61
Charborough, 35
Charles I, 3, 4, 8, 31
Charles II, 32
Charlton House, Kent, 7, 8, 26, 27
Charterhouse, London, 19, 27
Chatsworth, 18, 32–35, 37, 39–41, 60, 63
Cheere, Sir Henry and John, 55
Chelsea Hospital, 39
Chesterfield House, 45, 49
Chesterfield, Lord, 45, 49
Chiaroscuro, 62
Chicheley, Bucks.; 30, 51, 52, 62, 72, 158
Chief Groundes of Architecture, The, 1
Chimney-pieces
    Early Renaissance, 26–28; **4, 6, 25, 26, 29, 30**
    Late Stuart, 42, 43; **33, 42, 84**
    Early Georgian, 49, 54, 55; **84–86, 114–116**
    Classical Revival, 69–71; **168, 172**
    Regency and Revived Gothic, 74; **177, 192, 194**
        American, 49; **73, 74, 99, 101, 104**
        Armorial bearings, 2, 26; **2, 6, 25, 30**
        Bas-relief panels, 70, 71
        Carving, 19, 20, 38, 39, 43; **25, 26, 30**

Chimney-pieces—*continued*
    Caryatids, 20, 27, 42, 54
    Chinese taste, 55
    Coloured and gilded, 27, 55
    Consoles, 42, 54
    Corner fireplaces, 43
    Flemish influence, 6, 7
    Gothic, 55, 74; **192, 194**
    Grotesque ornament, 8; **29**
    Hooded, 25
    Inlay work, 20, 27
    Marble, 7, 26–28, 42, 43, 54, 55, 70, 71, 74; **4, 84**
    Ormolu decoration, 70
    Overpieces, 26, 27, 42, 52, 54
    Pilasters, 42, 54; **42, 47, 52, 114**
    Rococo, 55
    Scagliola, 67, 70
    Stone, 25, 27, 55; **25**
    Tin and pewter ornament, 70, 71
    Two-staged and 'continued', 26, 27, 42, 43, 54, 70; **4, 6, 25, 26, 29, 30, 84**
    Wedgwood ornament, 71
Chinese taste, 48, 52, 55, 60, 64, 75–78
    Staircases, 48; **112**
    Wall-paintings; **185–187**
    Wall-paper, 48, 77, 78; **170, 184**
Chippenham Hall, 38
Cipriani, 61, 63
Civil War Period, 4
Christ Church, Oxford, 66
Christchurch, Hampshire, 5, 77
Christ's College, Cambridge, 13
Clandon Park, 52
Classical Revival, 56–71
Claydon, 4, 48, 52, 66
Clermont, François, 51; **33**
Cleyn, 17
Clifford's Inn, *chimney-piece*, 43
Clough, Richard, 6
Cobbe, John, 22
Cobham Hall, Kent, 27
Cockerell, S. R.; **171**
Codrington Library, Oxford, 66
Coeck, Pieter, 19
Coke, Thomas, 45
Coleman-Hollister House, U.S.A.; **148**
Coleshill, Berkshire, 4, 36, 37, 41, 53; **36**
Colt, Maximilian, 7, 27
Colt Hoare, Sir Richard, 58
Columns, 66, 67; **127, 149, 154, 156, 159, 160**
Convocation House, Oxford, 8
Coombe Abbey, 37, 40; **53, 54**
Corfe Castle, 4
Cothele, 27
Cottingham, 75
Coult, Maximilian, *see* Colt
Courteenhall, Northants; **169**
Crawley House, Beds.; **174**
Crewe Hall, Cheshire, 30; **13**
Crichel House, Dorset; **115, 129, 131, 141, 142, 144, 157, 159, 166**
Cromwell House, Highgate, 25
Croome Court, 64, 69
Croscombe Church, 19
Crunden, John; **130**
Cuer, Cornelius and William, 7, 27

Cumberland House, 64
Cupola House, Carolina, U.S.A.; **73, 74**

Dalkeith Palace, 38, 43
Damini, Pietro, 34
Dance, George, 59, 65; **128**
Danckers, Hendrick, 33
Dangan, Richard, 22
Darly, Matthias, 64
Davis, *carver*, 40
Deal panelling, 18, 52
Dean Street, No. 75; Soho, **63**
Deare, John, 71
De Critz, 3, 4; **34**
De Gree, 62
Delvaux, Laurent, 54
Denham Place, 36; **61**
Derby House, London, 67, 70
Devon
    Carvings, 20
    Plasterwork, 23
Devonshire House, London, 53
Dilettanti Society, 46, 56–58
Dininckhoff, Bernard, 29; **31**
Ditchley, 46, 51, 54, 55; **94**
Ditterlein, 7
Dodington Park, 60; **133–135, 137, 147, 154, 160, 162**
Doors and Doorways
    Early Renaissance, 28, 29
    Late Stuart, 43, 44; **1, 14, 32, 76, 117**
    Early Georgian, 55; **83, 118–121**
    Classical Revival, 71; **166, 169**
    Regency and Revived Gothic; **182, 183**
        American examples; **80, 81, 101**
        Columns, 28, 43; **50**
        Overdoor panels, 43, 44, 52
        Panelling, 28, 29, 44, 72
        Pediments, 43, 55
Drakelowe, 36, 62
Drayton, Northants, 34, 36, 38, 65; **48**
Dublin
    Belvedere College, 69
    9 Henrietta Street; **107**
    32 St. Stephen's Green, 64
    17 St. Stephen's Square; **139**
    Trinity College; **86**
    Painted marble, 70
Dunster Castle; **39**
Dunsterfield, *plasterer*, 45
Dyrham Park; **47**

Eastbury, 47, 48, 77
Easton Neston, 36, 51; **70, 82, 117**
Eaton Hall, Cheshire, 75; **188, 189, 195**
Elements of Architecture, The, 4
Elizabethan period, 1, 2, 7, 8
Eltham, 41
Ely House, London, 59, 69
Emmett, William, 39
Empire Style, 74
Erddig, *panelling*, 38
Esher, *paintings by Kent*, 50
Etruscan style, 57, 67; **150**
Euston, 34, 38
Exeter, carvings at, 20

FAMBELER, Giles, 6
Fanelli, Francesco, 9
Farnham Chapel, 38
Fawley Court, 18
Fiennes, Diary of Celia, 33
Fireplaces see Chimney-pieces
Flaxman, as chimney-piece designer, 71
Flemish influence, 6–8, 26, 27, 29
Fonthill, 50, 70, 75
Forde Abbey, 22, 36, 41; 14
Foreign influences
    Chinese, 48, 52, 55, 60, 64, 75–78; 112, 170, 184–187
    Dutch, 31, 32
    Eastern, 2
    Etruscan, 57, 67; 150
    Flemish, 6, 7, 8, 19
    French, 9, 31, 32, 48, 49, 51, 52, 59, 73, 74
    Greek, 57–59, 73, 74
    Italian, 1–9, 45–48, 56–60
    Low Countries, 6–8, 26, 27, 29
    Venetian, 46
Foreign travel, 45, 46, 56–60
Fortrey, Samuel, 23
Fosse, Charles de la, 34
Fountains Abbey, 29
Franchini brothers, 5; 108
Friezes, 10, 16, 23, 38, 51, 63; 2, 42, 61, 85
Furniture, Empire style, 74

GABRIEL Hervey House, Wall-paintings, 11
Galleries, 3, 46, 47, 56; 4, 10, 64, 92, 126
Gawthorp House, 69
Gawthorpe Hall, 20, 23
Gedde, Walter, 29
Gibbons, Grinling, 39, 40, 43; 59, 78
Gibbs, James, 46, 54; 94, 95
Gilling Castle, Yorks., 10, 15, 20, 29; 2, 31
Gilpin, 63
Glazing, see Windows
Golden Cross Hotel, Oxford, 13
Goodwood House, Sussex; 87
Gorhambury, 29
Gothic Revival, 48, 75; 188–192, 194, 195
Gouge, Edward, 36, 37; 53
Grafton Street, No. 4, London, 65; 168
Graining of woodwork, 68
Grand Tour, 45, 46
Gravel Lane, Houndsditch, 23
Great Fulford, 15
Great St. Helen's, 22
Greek influence, 57–59, 73, 74
Greenwich Hospital, 35, 37
    Chapel, 66
Greenwich, Queen's House, 37, 42
Gresham, Sir Thomas, 6
Grimsthorpe, 32, 35
Grisaille, 62; 182
Grosvenor Square, No. 8, London, 69
Grotesques, 8, 9 (diagram), 18, 19, 26; 29
Grove House, Woodford Common, 10, 11
Grove, John, 37
Guicciardini, 6
Guildford Hospital, staircase, 25
Gunston Hall, U.S.A.; 100

HADDON Hall, 15, 17, 25, 29, 30
Hagley Hall, 51; 89, 91–93, 118, 119, 124
Halbert, plasterer, 45
Halnaker, 15
Ham House, 41, 42, 76, 77
Hamilton, Gavin, 58
Hamilton, Sir William, 57, 58
Hamilton, William, painter, 62
Hampton Court Palace,
    Carvings, 39
    Ceilings, 12, 21
    Corner fireplace, 43
    Italian influence, 6
    Overdoor pictures, 33
    Wall-hangings, 76, 77
    Wall-painting, 34, 35
    Windows, 29
Handrails, see Staircases
Harding, painter, 63
Hardwick Hall, 1, 12, 22, 23
Harewood House, 61, 62, 64, 65, 69; 127, 140, 152, 161
Harleian Collection, 47
Harrison, Dyrik, 6
Harvington Hall, 11
Hatchlands, 59
Hatfield, 6, 7, 25, 27; 7
Hawksmoor, Nicholas; 70, 117
Haydocke, Richard, 4
Haynes, wainscot, 37
Heath, John and Lawrence, 22
Heaton Park, 62, 63, 66, 68
Hengrave, 15
Henry VII tomb, 5
Henry VIII, 1, 5
Henryk, 6
Herringstone, 24
Hethe, John and Laurence, 22
Heveningham, 60, 62, 66, 67, 69; 149, 163
Hewell Hall, 36
Heythrop, 66, 70
Hill Hall, Essex, 11, 12
Hinchingbrooke, 33
Hoddesden, Rawdon House, 25, 19, 20
Holbein, Hans, 4, 5, 25, 27
Holcombe Court, 21
Holkham Hall, 46, 51, 54, 55, 57, 77; 85
Holland (and see Foreign Influences), 31, 32
Holland, Henry, 65, 67, 68, 70, 73; 172, 173, 182
Holland House, 13, 17, 20
Holme Lacy, 39, 40; 46
Holyrood House; 45
Hoocker, turner, 6
Hooke, Richard, 32 (footnote)
Hope Lodge, U.S.A.; 81
Hope, Thomas, 57, 58, 73, 74
Houghton Hall, 38, 46, 51, 54, 57, 77; 84
Household Furniture and Decoration, 74
Hovingham Hall, York, 50
Hursley, panelling, 39

IBBETSON, Julius Caesar, 62
Iconology, 61, 63
Inlays, 20, 21
Interior Porches, 27; 27
Ipswich, Old Neptune Inn, 14

Italian influence, 1–9, 45–48, 56–60

JACKSON, George, plasterer, 66
Jansen, Bernard, 7
Jenever, chimney-piece designer, 6
Jenkins, antiquary, 58
Jerathmael Bower's House, U.S.A.; 103
Jerusalem Chamber, Westminster, 17
John Brown House, Rhode Island, U.S.A.; 104
Jones, Inigo, 9, 31, 36, 37, 42, 46, 51, 52, 54; 33–35

KAUFFMANN, Angelica, 61
Kederminster Library, 12, 17; 12
Kedleston, 59, 61, 63–70, 71 (footnote)
Kendall, 75
Kenilworth, 2
Kenmore, U.S.A.; 44
Kennard, joiner, 33
Kensington Palace, 38, 39, 46, 50
Kent, William, 46, 50, 52, 54, 57, 75; 84, 85
Kenwood, 61, 62, 69
Kew Palace, 23, 48, 51, 52
Kimbolton, 32, 77
King's College Chapel, Cambridge, 5
Kirby Hall, 7, 36
Kirtlington, 51
Kiveton, 36
Knole, Kent
    Cartoon gallery; 4
    Carving of screen, 19, 30
    Ceilings, 22; 4
    Heating, 3
    Marble chimney-pieces, 7, 27; 4
    Staircase, 24

LABRIÈRE, artist, 68
Laguerre, 34; 41
Lambourn Hall, 20
Lamport Hall, 36
Langley Marish Church, 12, 17; 11, 12
Lanscroon, Gerrard, 33, 34; 69
Lansdowne Collection, 57, 58
Lansdowne House, 61; 128
Lavenham Guildhall, 13
Layer Marney Church, 5
Layer Marney Tower, 1
Le Roy, 58
Lee, Kent, 75
Lee House, U.S.A., 49
Lees Court, Kent, 4, 31; 24, 32
Leicester, Lord, 45
Leoni, 46
Levens, inlay work, 20
Leverton, Thomas, 59, 60, 65, 69
Libraries, 46, 47, 49, 75; 137, 181, 191, 192, 194, 195
Lichfield House, London, 62
Lightfoot, decorator, 48
Lincoln, John, 6
Linenfold panelling, 14
Little Moreton Hall, 23

Wainscot—*continued*
  Linenfold, 14 (*and footnote*)
  Lozenge design, 15
  Mahogany panelling, 52
  Medallioned heads, 14, 15
  Mouldings, 16, 17, 37, 38, 52
  Oak Panelling, 13, 15, 17, 18; **3, 5**
  Painted, 12, 13, 17, 37, 38, 52; **12, 56, 58**
  Picture panels, 37, 52; **78, 79**
  Pilaster divisions, 15–17, 37, 38; **15, 45, 47, 50, 51, 55, 77–79**
  Pine panelling, 37, 52
  Recessed panels, 37, 52
  Soft wood panelling, 18, 37, 52
  Strapwork, 8, 16, 19
  Walnut panelling, 18, 38
Wakefield, 32
Wall decoration (*see* Wall hangings, etc. *below, and* Plasterwork)
Wall hangings
  Regency period, 74, 76, 77
  Tapestries, 2, 3, 9, 76; **43, 49, 89, 118**
Wall paintings
  Early Renaissance, 9–12; **12, 21–23**
  Late Stuart, 33–36; **1, 56–58**
  Early Georgian, 50, 51
  Classical Revival, 60–64; **163, 172, 173, 182**
    American; **55**
    Apocryphal figures, 11; **21–23**
    Chinese taste; **185–187**
    Etruscan style, 67; **150**
    Panoramas, 62, 63
Wall-papers, 13, 48, 77, 78
  American use of, 49
  Chinese, 48, 77, 78; **170, 184**
  Egyptian; **174**
Walnut panelling, 18, 38
Walpole, Horace, 9, 40, 45, 57, 60, 62, 75
Waltham Abbey, 17

Wanstead, 47, 50, 78
War Office (Old), *staircase*, 69
Wardour Castle, 4
Ware, Isaac, 48, 49, 52, 54, 55
Warwick Castle; 38
Waterman House, U.S.A.; **101**
Watson, Samuel, 40
Watts, Christopher, 25
Weare Gifford, *frieze*, 23
Webb, John 4, 31, 36, 37, 42–44, 46; **35**
Wedgwood, Josiah, 57, 58, 71
Wentworth Castle; 40, 42
Wentworth Woodhouse, 52; **88, 90, 156**
West Hanningfield Meeting House, 12
West Hoathly Priest's House, 10
Weston, Sir Richard, 1
White Swan, Stratford-on-Avon, 11; **21–23**
Whitehall Banqueting House, 31
William III, 32
Williams, John, 22
Willoughby, Sir Francis, 1
Wilton House
  Ceilings, 31, 36; **33, 34**
  Chimney-pieces, 31, 42; **33**
  Colonnade Room; **33**
  Decorative painting, 34
  Doors, 43
  Double Cube Room, 31, 37, 42, 43; **34**
  Panelling, 37
  Single Cube Room, 31; **35**
Wilton, Joseph, 71
Wilsley House, Kent; **56**
Wimbledon Hall, 13
Wimpole Hall; **181**
Winchester, 5
Winchester College Chapel, 39
Winckelmann, 58
Winde, Capt. William, *see* Wynne
Windows
  Early Renaissance, 28, 29; **2, 31**

Windows—*continued*
  Cast Iron tracery, 75
  Coloured glass, 28, 29, 75; **2, 31**
Windsor Castle, 34, 39, 61, 71
Witt, Giles de, 7, 27
Withepole House, Ipswich, 77
Woburn Abbey, 73
Woodhall Park, 60, 67; **151**
Woodwork, *see* Carving, Wainscot, etc.
Wollaton Hall, 1, 7
Wolseley Hall, 40, 41
Wolsey, Cardinal, 1, 5
Wolterton, 54
Wood, John; **108**
Worsley, Sir Richard, 58
Wotton, Sir Henry, 4, 21, 24
Wotton-under-Edge, 78
Wren, Sir Christopher, 32
Wrought Iron, 41, 53, 69, 75; **70, 107, 154–156, 160, 161**
Wyatt, James, 59–62, 66, 71, 75
  Works illustrated:
    Ashridge House; **193**
    Crichel House; **141–144**
    Dodington Park: **133–135, 137, 147, 154, 160. 162**
    Heveningham; **149, 163**
Wyatt, Samuel; **155**
Wynne, Capt. William, 32; **54**

YARBOROUGH, Lord, 57
Yarnton, *chimney-piece*, 27
Yenn, *designer*, 64
York, *chimney-piece*; **26**

ZUCARELLI, 63
Zucchi, Antonio, 61, 63